TIME GAMBIT

MASTER THE MOVES THAT MAKE TIME WORK FOR YOU

BRENT WM. BAUER

TIME GAMBIT: Master the Moves That Make Time Work for You

For permission requests, contact:

Bauer Leadership Consulting Group, LLC
www.BauerLeadership.com
Email: support@TimeGambitBook.com

This is a work of nonfiction. Names, examples, and anecdotes may have been changed to protect privacy or used with permission. Any resemblance to actual persons, living or dead, or actual events is purely coincidental. The author and publisher have made every effort to ensure the accuracy of the information presented herein. However, they make no representations or warranties with respect to the completeness or applicability of the contents and disclaim any liability for any loss or damages arising from its use.

First Edition — 2026

Printed in the United States of America
ISBN (Hardback): 979-8-9939021-0-4
ISBN (Paperback): 979-8-9939021-1-1
ISBN (eBook): 979-8-9939021-3-5
ISBN (Audiobook): 979-8-9939021-5-9

Library of Congress Control Number: 2025949153
Published by **Bauer Leadership Consulting Group, LLC**

DEDICATION

To my children, Breanne and Brenden —

You have been both my reason and my reflection. In the early years, while you were growing and finding your way, I was doing the same. Many of the lessons that shaped Time Gambit were forged in that season: learning how to work with purpose, how to guard what matters most, and how to lead without losing myself in the noise.

Each principle in these pages carries a piece of that journey. My hope is that, as you face the challenges and opportunities of your own lives, these insights will give you a strategic advantage — helping you reach your goals with clarity, courage, and grace. And if they spare you even a few of the hard lessons that taught me, then this work will have done what it was meant to do.

May it also serve your children one day, as a reminder that time is not just to be managed, but mastered with meaning. I love you. -Dad

ACKNOWLEDGMENTS

To my wife, Freida — your steadfast support, patience, and faith have carried me through every uncertain step of this entrepreneurial journey. Building Bauer Leadership Consulting Group, LLC, and the ideas that eventually became Time Gambit, would not have been possible without your quiet strength and unwavering belief in me. You have sacrificed more than most will ever know, and I am endlessly grateful.

To Allan Wilson — your friendship and encouragement were instrumental in bringing this book to life. You saw the value in our work together and challenged me to share it more broadly, not for recognition, but to help others find the same clarity and focus you discovered. For that, and for your continued trust, I thank you deeply.

To the members of Advantage Alliances™ peer advisory groups— you have been both sounding board and inspiration. Though I have been tasked with facilitating your journeys together, I have learned as much, if not more, from each of you. Your insights, courage, and willingness to grow have sharpened my own understanding of leadership and time stewardship.

Finally, to the mentors, leaders, and associates who have influenced me over the past four decades — thank you. Whether you led with excellence or became a great model for what not-to-do in leadership, your examples, both good and imperfect, shaped the man and coach I have become. The cumulative value from every lesson, every encounter, has influenced what appears in these pages. For that, I am profoundly grateful.

TABLE OF CONTENT

Time /tīm/
The indefinite, continuous progression of existence and events from the past through the present, into the future; a measurable period during which an action, process, or condition exists or continues.

Gam·bit /ˈgambət/
A calculated move, remark, or action intended to gain an advantage, often by taking a risk or making a sacrifice upfront.

TIME GAMBIT [The Arena & The Strategy]
A strategic move within the flow of time, where choices, risks, and sacrifices shape the trajectory of success.

PREFACE

Twenty something years ago, I found myself at a crossroads—a moment that would quietly, then unmistakably, reshape my future. I was transitioning back into a production management role after six years of fulfilling philanthropic work. On paper, it was a step forward. But internally, it felt like retreat. The new role came with a flashy title and broader scope, but my sense of meaning was unraveling. I felt like I was betraying something.

One Monday morning, I sat at my desk, staring at a dark computer monitor, unable to move. I felt flat; disconnected; empty. Somewhere in the numbness, a question slipped from my lips before I could stop it: "What am I doing here?"

A colleague outside my office replied, "Are you talkin' to me?"

That awkward moment was also a holy one. It laid bare the dissonance I'd been carrying for months. I wasn't just drifting—I was sinking. The most alive parts of me were fading under the weight of obligation and misalignment. I hadn't yet named it, but I was beginning to feel the cost of time misused.

Around that time, I came across a story I've never forgotten. A traveler in Tuscany had pulled off the road near a vineyard. Wandering along the fence line, he noticed clusters of ripe grapes—so full they had begun to drop to the ground. Some were already spoiling in the dirt.

Something about that image hit me hard.

He said the scene brought to mind the Latin phrase Carpe Diem— loosely translated: "Seize the day." But standing there, looking at all that spoilinged fruit, he realized the phrase meant something deeper. It wasn't just a call to be bold. It was a warning:

Don't wait too long. The harvest won't keep.

That metaphor has stayed with me all these years later.

Opportunities don't last forever. They don't stand still and wait for you to get your act together. They ripen. And then they can either be seized or they rot. We may think we can pick up later where we failed to begin now, but opportunities can be few and far between. The same one will never come again. Once the muse strikes, if not grabbed, she will vanish into the stuff of dreams and imagination. Nothing tangible, just a remembered thought that is now just a whisper in the past.

What stayed with me wasn't just the scene—but the ache beneath it:

How often do we assume we'll have more time? More clarity? Another chance?

The truth is, time—life—doesn't stop. And it doesn't wait. It moves regardless of what it's made of.

We like to imagine we'll act when the moment is right. But the longer we wait, the more our best possibilities slip quietly past—unseen, unclaimed, wasted.

The vineyard reminded me that time is precious, fragile, and fleeting. The very things we hope to harvest—joy, growth, impact—can spoil right at our feet if we don't learn to recognize them and act.

As a business coach, I've since seen this struggle replicated in hundreds of lives—leaders, founders, and high-performers buried in the businesses they'd built, trading away their most valuable resource—time—for tasks, meetings, and false urgencies that never seem to end.

They aren't lazy. They aren't clueless. They're simply out of rhythm. Their calendars are full. Their potential is capped.

And that's where this book enters.

INTRODUCTION

THE VINEYARD AND THE GAMEBOARD

The vineyard taught me that timing matters. But it was a different metaphor—a gambit—that helped me see the solution.

In chess, a gambit is an intentional sacrifice—a pawn offered up early to gain an advantage later. Business, when played well, works the same way. You trade lower-value activities today for strategic positioning tomorrow. You give up comfort to gain clarity. You relinquish control to gain capacity.

> *You don't need more time. You need to master the moves that make time work for you.*

This book is about making those moves.

It's not a collection of productivity hacks. It's a new way to think about time—your most nonrenewable asset—and how to deploy it in ways that multiply your impact, not just your activity.

You'll learn how to:

- Identify and eliminate the subtle time thieves that erode your focus
- Build structures that protect your energy and unlock strategic clarity
- Reclaim your best hours for your highest priorities
- Shift from reactive busyness to proactive leadership

Along the way, I'll share real-world stories, practical frameworks, and field-tested tools I've used with leaders across industries who were ready to stop reacting—and start leading with purpose again.

WHY THE TIME GAMBIT MATTERS

Most people don't run out of time. They just stop directing it.

Leaders who learn to steward their time well become the kind of leaders others want to follow. They're calm under pressure. Clear on priorities. Creative again. Courageous again. With the enthusiasm of youth tempered by the wisdom of experience.

> *Most time problems are actually clarity problems in disguise.*

If you've ever felt like you're stuck in motion but not making progress—this book is for you.

If you've been running fast but unsure where you're going— this book is for you.

And if you're ready to trade exhaustion for intention and regain the upper hand on your calendar, your energy, and your leadership—then welcome.

> *When you learn to master time, you unlock more than hours—you unlock margin, meaning, and momentum.*

This book was intentionally crafted for the rhythm of your real life. With twenty chapters plus an introduction and conclusion, it's built for a 22-day journey—one chapter per business day over the course of a month.

Whether you read it quietly each morning before your day begins, or reflect on the questions in the evening after the dust settles, the goal is not to rush. It's to reflect. The seven calibration questions at the end of each chapter are where the real value is mined. Don't skip them. They are the levers that will multiply your return on time invested—and you won't need to give up your weekends to make it happen.

Let's begin the game.

Your next move starts here.

GET THE TIME GAMBIT TOOLBOX

To help you get the most out of this book, I've created the Time Gambit Toolbox— a curated set of worksheets, templates, and practical tools that pair with the key ideas in each chapter. These resources make it easier to move from reading to real-world application, giving you the structure and clarity to put each principle into practice.

For a limited window, I'm making the entire Toolbox available at no cost to readers of this edition. To receive your own Time Gambit Toolbox, simply email: support@timegambitbook.com with "Toolbox Access" in the subject line.

PART ONE
MAPPING TIME TRAPS

1 THE MYTH OF THE MULTITASKING MASTER

"TO DO TWO THINGS AT ONCE IS TO DO NEITHER."

- PUBLILIUS SYRUS -

Picture this: you're at your desk, juggling a phone call while scrolling through emails. Your calendar pings with a reminder, and before you know it, you're switching to another task, only to circle back to the first one moments later. By the end of the day, you feel exhausted but can't point to any meaningful progress. You were so productive at being unproductive, it might qualify as a skill set. Does this sound familiar? If so, you may have fallen for one of the most pervasive myths in modern business: the myth of the multitasking master.

At first glance, multitasking feels productive. You're busy, your schedule is packed, and you're handling a little bit of everything. But underneath the surface lies a harsh truth: multitasking isn't making you more efficient—it's robbing you of your focus, your energy, and ultimately, your time.

In this chapter we will uncover how multitasking undermines your productivity and explore how aligning your time and energy with your overarching purpose can transform both your business and your life.

ARE YOU REALLY GETTING MORE DONE?

Ask yourself: "When was the last time I felt truly in flow: "in the zone"? A time when I was so absorbed in a single task that hours passed like minutes, and the work I produced felt inspired and meaningful?" Now think about how often you're able to access that state. If the answer is "rarely" or "never," multitasking may be to blame.

Flow States: How the Mind Minimizes Energy Output to Put You in the Zone In this state, the brain minimizes energy output. You might think it would be the opposite: you're so focused on a task or activity that it must take more energy, right?

Not so. We've all had moments of genius, where an idea neatly flows into implementation and successful completion, where we become completely absorbed in a task or project. Creative ideas come through sometimes without planning and everything seems to happen in slow motion. This is common among artists, musicians, dancers, writers, speakers, and some athletes such as skiers and footballers.

Unfortunately, we can't be in a flow state all the time. If we were, our brains would not be able to make evaluations and decisions, solve problems or analyze information. Many artistic types who spend much of their time in flow don't see the value of managing the rest of their life. Grooming and household chores are mundane and tedious to them and anything to do with the business end of their endeavors is lost.

The prefrontal cortex of our brain governs problem solving, data collection, pattern recognition, planning, thought analysis, risk-reward assessment, will power, urge suppression, moral decisions, and evaluating and benefiting from experience. When you get into a flow state naturally because your only motivation is being completely involved in the activity for its own sake, the brain turns off some of its features, including the prefrontal cortex, literally freeing mental bandwidth so you get laser focus. This is called transient or temporary hypo-frontality.

Your sense of self is not active, and you begin to merge your awareness of the action with the action itself. You lose all self-consciousness and personal reflection. You don't self-monitor as you go along because your logical linear mind is turned off. You don't try to think yourself through the next move. You effortlessly choose in each moment and make adjustments and course corrections simultaneously as you work. You're in the zone.

The science is clear: the human brain is not designed for multitasking. When we attempt to handle multiple tasks simultaneously, we're not really doing them at the same time.

Instead, our brain rapidly shifts focus from one task to another, a process that comes with significant costs.

Dr. John Medina, author of Brain Rules, explains it like this: "The brain's attentional system is not capable of true multitasking. When people think they're multitasking, they're actually switching from one task to another very rapidly. And every time they do, there's a cognitive cost." This cost—known as "task-switching cost"—means that each time you redirect your focus, you lose time and mental energy.

One pivotal study conducted by researchers at the University of Michigan found that switching between tasks can reduce productivity by up to 40%. Think about that: for every ten hours you spend multitasking, four of them are essentially wasted. How many hours of your day could you reclaim if you stopped trying to "do it all"?

THE BRAIN VS. MULTITASKING

To understand why multitasking fails, let's take a closer look at how your brain operates. Your prefrontal cortex—the part of your brain responsible for decision-making, focus, and problem-solving—works best when it's allowed to focus on one task at a time.

When you force it to juggle multiple priorities, it becomes overwhelmed, like an overloaded computer that slows to a crawl.

A study by neuroscientist Dr. Earl Miller at MIT revealed that the prefrontal cortex struggles to process more than one high-level task simultaneously. While your brain can manage simple activities—like walking and talking at the same time—it's not equipped to handle complex tasks concurrently. For example, reading an email while participating in a video conference leads to diminished comprehension of both.

Even more concerning, multitasking triggers the release of stress hormones like cortisol. This fight-or-flight response may keep you alert in the short term, but over time, it depletes your energy reserves and impairs your ability to think clearly. Chronic multitaskers often report higher levels of anxiety and burnout, leaving them feeling stuck in a cycle of busywork that produces diminishing returns. Put another way:

> *Multitaskers burn twice the fuel to get half*
> *as far—and then wonder why*
> *they're always running on empty.*

Does any of this resonate with you? If so, consider this: what is multitasking costing you—not just in terms of productivity and energy, but in your ability to lead effectively, connect meaningfully with others, and align your actions with your greater purpose?

THE REAL-LIFE COST OF DOING IT ALL: EMILY'S STORY

Emily was the CEO of a thriving marketing firm. Her days were packed from dawn to dusk with meetings, emails, and problem-solving sessions. She prided herself on her ability to handle it all and wore her "multitasking prowess" like a badge of honor. But beneath the surface, Emily was struggling.

Her team began to notice cracks. Deadlines were slipping. Decisions were rushed. Important client relationships were strained. Despite working 12-hour days, Emily felt like she was accomplishing less and less. Sound familiar?

In a desperate attempt to regain control, Emily began tracking her time. What she discovered shocked her: more than six hours of her day were spent switching between tasks. Emails, text messages, and impromptu meetings constantly disrupted her focus, leaving her mentally drained, emotionally frustrated, short tempered, and unable to give her full creative attention to any task.

A business coach introduced Emily to the concept of "time blocking," a strategy that involves dedicating specific blocks of time to focused work. Emily began setting aside her mornings for strategic planning, scheduling all meetings for the afternoon, and limiting her email responses to a designated time slot each evening. She also instituted a "no interruptions" policy during her focus blocks, empowering her team to batch non-urgent questions.

Within weeks, Emily experienced a profound shift. Her productivity increased by 30%. Deadlines were met, client satisfaction improved, and her team's morale began to soar. For the first time in years, Emily felt in control of her time and energy. Her story is a testament to the transformative power of breaking free from the multitasking myth.

Now ask yourself: "Could my own "plate-spinning" tendencies be holding me back? What might change if I gave myself permission to focus on one thing at a time?"

ALIGNING TIME WITH PURPOSE

The myth of the multitasking master is seductive because it feeds our desire to achieve more, faster. But as Emily's story shows, true productivity isn't about doing more; it's about doing what matters most.

This principle lies at the heart of what I call Strategic TimeCasting.©

> *Strategic TimeCasting© is the practice of aligning your use of time and energy with the overarching purpose, vision, and values of your business.*

When you're in alignment, every hour you spend contributes to something meaningful. You're not just crossing items off a to-do list—you're building a business and a life that reflects your highest priorities.

To achieve Strategic TimeCasting©, start by asking yourself three powerful questions:

1. What is my highest priority right now? Identify the one task or goal that will make the biggest impact on your business and life.
2. Am I spending my time and energy in alignment with my values? Reflect on whether your daily actions support your long-term vision.
3. What can I eliminate or delegate to create more space for focused work? Consider which tasks are distracting you from what should be your true priorities.

By answering these questions honestly, you can begin to reclaim your time and direct your energy toward what truly matters.

REALITY CHECK

As a business owner, you hold the vision for your company. You set the pace, and your team looks to you for direction. If you're caught in the trap of multitasking, you're not just compromising your own effectiveness—you're impacting the entire organization.

So, I challenge you: take an honest look at how you're spending your time. What myths are you believing about your productivity? What would it look like to embrace a new way of working—one that prioritizes focus, purpose, and alignment?

The journey to Strategic TimeCasting© begins with a single step: the decision to stop chasing the illusion of multitasking mastery and start living and working with intentionality. The Strategic TimeCasting Worksheet© can be found in the Time Gambit Toolbox.

In the next chapter, we'll explore specific strategies to help you break free from time traps and design a schedule that aligns with your goals. But for now, remember:

> *The most important work you can do*
> *is the work that matters most.*

CALIBRATION QUESTIONS

1. When during your day do you feel the busiest—but accomplish the least? What's happening in those moments?
   → *Helps surface how perceived productivity may actually be scattered attention.*

THE MYTH OF THE MULTITASKING MASTER

2. What types of tasks do you typically try to handle at the same time? How confident are you in the quality of your output during those moments?
→ *Reveals where task-switching may be undermining effectiveness.*

3. How often do you find yourself mentally jumping between email, messages, and meetings—and what's the emotional toll?
→ *Brings awareness to the stress caused by constant switching.*

4. Can you remember the last time you were fully immersed in one task? What made that experience possible—and rare?
→ *Illuminates how infrequently "deep work" occurs.*

5. What tasks or conversations have suffered because your attention was divided?
→ *Invites reflection on real-world consequences of multitasking.*

6. Where in your schedule are you reacting instead of intentionally focusing?
→ *Encourages identification of chaotic, unstructured blocks of time.*

7. If someone shadowed you for a day, would they describe your work as focused and strategic—or fragmented and reactionary? Why?
→ *Prompts an externalized self-assessment that cuts through internal justification.*

*"Multitasking doesn't make you a master—
it makes you a magician who loses the rabbit and
forgets where you put the hat."*

RECOMMENDED RESOURCES

1. **Deep Work by Cal Newport**
   This book introduces the concept of "deep work" as the antidote to the distraction economy. Newport outlines how focus is a rare, valuable skill that drives meaningful productivity. It supports the chapter's argument that shallow multitasking erodes performance and clarity.

2. **The One Thing by Gary Keller & Jay Papasan**
   Keller emphasizes that success comes not from doing more, but from doing the right thing—one thing—at a time. The book offers practical strategies for reducing distractions and achieving focused execution. It echoes the chapter's challenge to stop juggling and start prioritizing.

3. **Essentialism by Greg McKeown**
   McKeown advocates for "the disciplined pursuit of less." His framework urges readers to eliminate the trivial many in favor of the vital few—reinforcing the chapter's call to align time with values and purpose, not just busyness.

4. **Brain Rules by Dr. John Medina**
   This science-based guide explains why the brain struggles with multitasking. Medina's work is directly cited in the chapter and provides foundational neuroscience behind task-switching costs and diminished focus.

5. **Stolen Focus by Johann Hari**
   Hari explores why attention is collapsing—personally and culturally—and what can be done to restore it. It expands on the chapter's themes by adding societal context to personal struggles with attention and energy depletion.

6. **Focus on This by Full Focus (Michael Hyatt & team)**
   A podcast focused on practical productivity through single-tasking and calendar control. Each episode reinforces time-blocking, goal alignment, and the myth of multitasking with digestible tactics. Pairs well with the worksheet's focus block design.

7. **The Productivity Show by Asian Efficiency**
   This podcast blends neuroscience, tools, and habits to improve focus and intentionality. It frequently discusses how to reduce decision fatigue and eliminate distractions—concepts echoed in Chapter 1 of Time Gambit.

8. **Cal Newport's Deep Questions Podcast**
   Hosted by the author of Deep Work, this podcast unpacks digital minimalism, cognitive load, and the costs of scattered attention. It's a great companion to the science-based arguments in the chapter.

9. **Why Multitasking is Killing Your Productivity – Harvard Business Review**
   This well-researched article summarizes academic findings on the cognitive cost of task switching. It validates the claims made in Chapter 1 with corporate credibility and peer-reviewed evidence.

10. **Zen Habits Blog by Leo Babauta**
    Babauta writes elegantly about mindfulness, simplicity, and doing less better. His posts often address how to resist distraction and embrace slower, more intentional work rhythms.

11. James Clear's Blog
Clear's articles explore behavior change, habit design, and the power of attention. His writing supports the worksheet's approach to identifying triggers and shifting toward high-leverage tasks.

12. The Cost of Interrupted Work – American Psychological Association
This piece explains how interruptions—not just multitasking—cause long recovery times and productivity loss. It reinforces the chapter's insight that even attempted multitasking pulls energy away from meaningful progress.

2 | MEETING OVERLOAD

"A MEETING IS AN EVENT AT WHICH THE MINUTES ARE KEPT, AND THE HOURS ARE LOST."

- ANON -

RECLAIMING YOUR TIME WITH PURPOSEFUL MEETINGS

Meetings are supposed to be engines of progress—but let's be honest: they often become speed bumps instead. You walk into the day with energy and intention. Then the meetings start. One after another, back-to-back. By noon, your focus is scattered. By evening, your to-do list is still taunting you from the corner of your desk. And the creeping thought returns: "Did I actually move the needle today?"

Somewhere between your third coffee and fourth calendar invite, you may have become a professional 'meeting attender' with a side hustle in actual work.

This isn't just about lost time—it's about lost opportunity. Every hour in a poorly run meeting is an hour not spent on strategy, growth, or real problem-solving. If your calendar is jammed with meetings, you're not leading—you're juggling.

And leadership isn't about keeping everything in the air. It's about knowing what's worth catching.

There is always someone who dominates the room when questions are asked, and there are always those who make no effort to give input. You don't need to abolish meetings. You need to reclaim them. Refocus them. Transform them into what they were meant to be: precise tools for alignment and action. Meetings should serve the mission—not sabotage it. But that only happens when the leader sets the tone.

> *In the race of business, extra laps around the conference table don't count.*

THE TRUE COST OF INEFFECTIVE MEETINGS

The real danger of meeting overload isn't just that it eats up hours, it's that it slowly erodes the core of your business—your intention and direction. Time that should be spent advancing key initiatives gets swallowed by conversations that go nowhere. Decision-makers leave with less clarity, not more. Teams grow weary of the cycle, and leadership ends up reacting instead of driving. To fix it, you have to see it for what it really is: a leak in the hull that's sinking your ship, one drip at a time.

- **Wasted Time:** Meetings without a clear agenda spiral into circular conversations and drain valuable hours. Every minute spent talking in circles is a minute stolen from focused execution. Left unchecked, this becomes an organizational habit that kills momentum and diminishes enthusiasm and creativity.

- **Decision Fatigue:** Leaving a meeting with more questions than answers isn't just frustrating—it's costly. When leaders are forced to constantly revisit decisions or shoulder every choice themselves, their cognitive load skyrockets. The result? Slower thinking, poorer judgment, and risk of burnout.

- **Productivity Drain:** Long-winded meetings don't just run over—they run roughshod over your priorities. When meetings intrude on peak work time, they fracture attention and make deep work nearly impossible. Projects stall not because of lack of talent, but lack of uninterrupted time.

- **Disengaged Employees:** Forcing team members into irrelevant meetings signals that their time doesn't matter. Over time, this leads to disengagement, apathy, and erosion of trust. People stop contributing not because they don't care, but because they stop believing it makes a difference.

- **Financial Impact:** Ten people in a one-hour meeting at $100K salaries? That's $500 in labor cost—gone. Multiply that by dozens of meetings a week, and you're burning through capital without a single measurable return. And that does not take into account time spent by each team member in refocusing on their actual work. Meeting bloat is not just a cultural issue—it's a financial one.

Recognizing these costs is only the first step. The next step? Implementing simple but effective strategies to ensure meetings are fewer, shorter, and results-driven.

SIGNS YOUR MEETINGS ARE DRAINING TIME

Many business leaders don't recognize the true impact of ineffective meetings because they are deeply ingrained in their daily routines. The normalization of excessive meetings can make it difficult to see how much time is actually being lost. Leaders often assume meetings are necessary for collaboration and decision-making, but without a clear structure, they can quickly become counterproductive.

> *Activity does not equal productivity.*

A calendar full of meetings gives the illusion of importance and engagement, but in reality, it often means that high-value work is being neglected. Leaders who spend their days bouncing between meetings may feel like they are contributing, but without focused execution time, real progress is stalled.

Additionally, many leaders (especially those who have built the business from scratch) struggle with delegation which results in them attending meetings that they don't need to be a part of. Instead of empowering their teams to make decisions independently, they insert themselves into every discussion, adding unnecessary layers of approval and slowing down workflows. This not only drains their own time but also disempowers their employees, creating a culture of dependency instead of efficiency.

Fear of missing out (FOMO) is another phrase for micromanaging your team. If you feel compelled to attend every meeting to stay informed or maintain control, you're micromanaging. This is a poor leadership habit that leads to decision fatigue and contributes to burnout. Things often change quickly. Trying to stay on top of everything is almost impossible. Trusting the right people to handle discussions and only participating in high-impact meetings is a necessary shift for sustainable leadership. Don't worry. If you have a good team in place, major decisions won't be made without your input.

This isn't about working harder—it's about working smarter. The solution? Take control of your meetings before they control you.

RULES FOR EFFECTIVE MEETINGS & TIME-BLOCKING STRATEGIES

The reality is, most leaders don't set out to have their schedules hijacked by meetings. It happens gradually, as what are often self-imposed demands on their time increase and well-intended discussions morph into recurring obligations. What starts as a tool for collaboration turns into a treadmill of endless conversations, leaving far less room for meaningful work. This isn't just a problem for the leader—it's a problem created by the leader, and it almost always cascades throughout the entire organization.

Employees take their cues from leadership. If meetings dominate the calendar of an owner, CEO, or senior manager, the rest of the team assumes that's the standard expectation. Before long, everyone is caught in the same cycle— overbooked, overstretched, and underproductive—with lots of interruptions that take them away from what should be their main focus. Worse, an unexamined meeting culture stifles the autonomy and creativity of the team, forcing every decision through layers of discussion instead of empowering employees to act.

Breaking free from this pattern requires a shift in perspective. Instead of seeing meetings as a necessary evil, leaders must redefine them as strategic tools—used only when they add value, structured for efficiency, and never allowed to disrupt the real work of the business. The following principles will help you implement this shift and reclaim your time.

To make meetings work for you, consider using The Table Rule™ method:

The Table Rule – Only the essential get a seat– every seat has a reason to attend.

1. **Pinpoint the Purpose**
   If a meeting doesn't have a clear and compelling reason, it doesn't belong on the calendar. What's the outcome you're driving toward? No purpose? No meeting. This might seem obvious, but you'd be surprised how many meetings are scheduled for unnecessary "updates" because a leader feels the need to be kept in the loop on every bit of minutia.

2. **Keep It Crisp**
   Target 15 to 30 minutes—tight, focused, and prepared. When meetings stretch past their welcome, it's often due

to a preparation failure. Fifteen minutes may not seem like much time. Even 30 minutes can go by quickly, so it's vital to inform attendees that this is not the time for gossip, chair shuffling, or bringing up items that don't pertain to the meeting agenda.

3. **Filter the Faces**
   Invite only the voices vital to the decision at hand. The fewer the attendees, the sharper the outcomes. Don't allow one person (and there's always one) to dominate the room unless they are key to this decision.

4. **Anchor the Agenda**
   Send a clear, structured agenda in advance—discussion points, time limits, and expected decisions. The agenda is your guardrail against drift.

5. **Reserve as a Last Resort**
   Not every conversation deserves a conference room. If it can be handled in a message or a quick call, skip the meeting.

6. **Protect Prime Hours**
   Mornings are for momentum. Defend your deep work blocks and make them immovable—your calendar should serve your priorities, not sabotage them.

TAKE BACK YOUR TIME

Meetings should move the mission forward—not muddy the waters. They're meant to create clarity, alignment, and momentum—not become a bureaucratic bottleneck. When you take ownership of when, why, and how meetings happen, you're not just reclaiming hours—you're reclaiming impact and improving employee motivation and morale.

And here's the truth: organizational culture doesn't shift until leaders do. If you want a team that values focus, speed, and progress, it won't come from another memo. It starts with your calendar. It starts with your example.

> *Every meeting you redesign is a message to your team: Time matters here.*

CALIBRATION QUESTIONS

1. How often do your meetings produce clear, actionable results?
   → *Prompts a check-in on effectiveness versus effort expended.*

2. What percentage of your meetings could have been handled through email or a quick call?

→ *Reveals potential for reducing unnecessary meeting volume.*

3. How could your meetings be better structured to maximize engagement and minimize wasted time?

→ *Encourages strategic thinking around agendas, pacing, and facilitation.*

4. As a leader, how are you modeling effective time management for your team?

→ *Links personal behavior to team-wide time culture.*

5. What small changes could you make this week to reduce meeting overload?
→ *Shifts focus to immediate, practical action.*

6. Where in your calendar have meetings encroached on your deep work time?
→ *Highlights scheduling conflicts that sabotage strategic focus.*

7. Who on your team could handle a meeting you currently attend—and what's stopping you from handing it off?
→ *Invites reflection on trust, delegation, and leadership maturity.*

> *If your answers stung a bit, it's not failure*
> *talking—that's focus showing up.*

FINAL THOUGHTS

If there's one thing a bloated meeting culture reveals, it's a leadership team that hasn't drawn the line between collaboration and control. Meetings are necessary—at times, even catalytic—but when they multiply without discipline, they don't just waste time. They dilute clarity. They pull your best people away from the work that actually moves the business forward.

And it doesn't stop with you. Your calendar sends a message. When every decision is processed through a roomful of people, your team learns to wait. When your schedule is wall-to-wall meetings, they assume that's how success is measured. Eventually, everyone's just busy—without being productive.

This chapter isn't about eliminating meetings. It's about restoring their purpose. It's about creating a structure where time is respected, decisions are clean, and the team learns to act—not wait for permission. And that starts with the person who sets the tone.

Look at your calendar. Then look at your team. If you don't like what you see in either place, you know where to start.

RECOMMENDED RESOURCES

1. **The Surprising Science of Meetings: How You Can Lead Your Team to Peak Performance** by Steven G. Rogelberg
This book is grounded in real organizational research and offers science-backed strategies for making meetings more effective. It reinforces many of the themes from this chapter, such as limiting attendees, setting clear agendas, and rethinking meeting norms—making it a perfect follow-up for leaders ready to challenge the status quo.

2. **Death by Meeting: A Leadership Fable...About Solving the Most Painful Problem in Business** by Patrick Lencioni
Told as a business fable, this book brings the pain of ineffective meetings to life through storytelling. Lencioni offers a framework that aligns with the idea of using meetings intentionally and distinguishing between different types of meetings—reinforcing the chapter's focus on purpose-driven structure.

3. **Running Effective Meetings For Dummies** by Joseph A. Allen and Karin M. Reed
This is a tactical, user-friendly resource that complements the practical tips in this chapter. If you're looking for checklists, how-to advice, and a down-to-earth tone, this guide provides step-by-step solutions for every kind of meeting scenario.

4. **Meetings Suck: Turning One of The Most Loathed Elements of Business into One of the Most Valuable** by Cameron Herold

Herold makes the case that meetings don't inherently suck—we just run them badly. His perspective echoes the transformation mindset encouraged in this chapter and will help you see meetings as a skill you and your team can develop to gain real strategic advantage.

5. **When: The Scientific Secrets of Perfect Timing** by Daniel H. Pink

While not specifically about meetings, this book adds nuance to the idea of time-blocking. Pink explores how our productivity fluctuates throughout the day, supporting the suggestion that leaders should reserve their peak energy hours for deep work and strategic thinking—not meetings.

6. **Time Wasted In Meetings: 59+ Meeting Statistics**
@ CrossRiverTherapy.com

This article compiles compelling data points that support the chapter's warning about the hidden cost of unproductive meetings. If you're looking to reinforce the business case with numbers, this is a great place to start.

7. **Time Wasted In Meetings: 30 Meeting Statistics**
@ GoldenStepsABA.com

Another excellent data-driven resource that highlights how prevalent and costly meeting inefficiency is. These statistics validate the idea that meeting reform isn't just a leadership preference—it's a bottom-line business need.

8. **19 Best Running Meetings Books of All Time** @ MeetingScience.io
   If this chapter sparked your interest and you want to go even deeper, this curated list pulls together some of the top books available on running better meetings. It's a solid starting point for building a meeting-savvy leadership library.

3 | COMMUNICATION CHAOS

"TIME IS WHAT WE WANT MOST BUT WHAT WE USE WORST."

– WILLIAM PENN –

Founder of Pennsylvania

ATTENTION TO EMAIL

You sit down, ready to conquer something important—then ding. An email wants a moment of your time. You open it, dash off a reply, and another one swoops in. Ten minutes later, you're still swatting at the swarm. The real work? Still waiting patiently in the background, arms crossed. Once again, your inbox has staged a hostile takeover of your day.

Emails pull you into conversations that rarely deserve the red-carpet treatment. What begins as a "quick check" quietly morphs into an hour-long detour. The urgent gets postponed. By day's end, you've been busy, yes, but with things that bear little resemblance to productivity—like running on a treadmill set to "reply all." Incoming messages have multiplied like rabbits; critical thinking has given way to what you've now deemed a priority—whether you're aware of it or not—and that has left you chasing smoke. In essence, you've been conducting an impromptu email meeting—unplanned, unscheduled, and unnecessary.

Every ping steals your focus and forces your brain to shift gears. As we touched on in Chapter 1, that switch comes with a toll. It's not the email that's expensive—it's the recovery time. Many leaders suffer under the tyranny of reactivity, but just as in so many other aspects of leading well, freedom begins with awareness.

> *Email is a tool—not your boss.*

When you begin to curb your email habits, you reclaim time that actually matters. This isn't about becoming an email minimalist—it's about keeping email in its proper lane.

Left unchecked, your attention to email becomes the perfect disguise for procrastination. You feel productive replying to bite-sized requests, but the real progress—strategic work—gets crowded out. The inbox becomes a sanctuary for avoidance, wrapped in a productivity costume.

And thanks to technology, that temptation is always within arm's reach. Your phone pings while you're in line for coffee. It buzzes mid-meeting. It even taps on your shoulder when you should be listening to your kid. But real efficiency isn't about always being available—it's about knowing when not to be.

Email plays a role in communication, but it should not be the centerpiece of your day. Strategic thinking, problem-solving, and leadership require sustained focus. Limiting email distractions allows for deeper concentration and better decision-making.

You can't lead from your inbox—
it's a communication channel,
not a command center.

THE TIME LEADERS LOSE TO EMAIL

The numbers tell a sobering truth: leaders spend an average of 28% of their workweek on email—more than eleven hours sorting, scanning, and sending. And that's before factoring in the hidden cost: the time it takes to refocus after each interruption.

According to a Harvard Business Review study, professionals check email fifteen times a day—roughly once every thirty-seven minutes. That's not communication—it's compulsion. Each check yanks you out of your zone and drops you into a whirlpool of low-value tasks disguised as "staying on top of things."

And it gets worse. Research shows it takes about twenty-three minutes to recover full focus after an interruption. Stack that across a day of ping-driven decision detours, and you're not working—you're ricocheting.

The damage isn't confined to business hours either. Many leaders check emails late at night, early in the morning, or in those in-between moments that should belong to their families—or their peace of mind. The result? Always on. Never really off.

Breaking this pattern begins with giving yourself permission—permission to be unavailable. When leaders reclaim their attention, they reclaim their time. Fewer interruptions mean sharper thinking and more meaningful progress.

The pressure to reply instantly is self-inflicted—and contagious.

- Most messages don't require immediate action, but without guardrails, urgency becomes the default.
- Set expectations with your team. Create breathing room. Thoughtful communication isn't slower—it's smarter.

WHEN I RAN THE NUMBERS FOR A ROOM FULL OF BUSINESS OWNERS...

Inbox clutter isn't just visual noise—it's mental weight. The pile-up creates a chronic sense of incompleteness. A clean inbox doesn't just look better. It feels better. And it frees your focus for the work that actually matters.

A few years back, I launched a one-day workshop for business owners called GAMEPLAN, where we tackled many of the themes you're reading about now—including the chaos email can create. One element that really seemed to bring the point home to those in attendance was an exercise that had wheels spinning for everyone in the room. Here is what I asked them to consider:

To drive the point home, I walked participants through a simple math exercise. And when the numbers hit the screen, you could practically hear the gears grinding in the room. Here's what I asked them to consider:

If you spend just 10 minutes every hour tending your inbox...

- That's 80 minutes per day (on an 8-hour schedule)
- Which becomes 6.66 hours per week
- Then scales to nearly 29 hours a month
- Which adds up to 346+ hours per year

That's the equivalent of two full work months—vanished.

Two months of potential strategy, momentum, margin, or creativity—spent playing digital ping-pong with your inbox. Most people wouldn't even take a vacation that long.

Now, consider that I was working with rounded numbers to make the math a little easier. The studies I referred to earlier actually reflect something a little more than 11 hours per week devoted to email.

> *If email were an employee, it would be your most expensive underperformer— eating up hours, dodging accountability, and never quite delivering results.*

INBOX ZERO, BATCHING, AND COMMUNICATION PROTOCOLS

Inbox Zero isn't about perfection—it's about decisiveness. A clutter-free inbox keeps messages from stacking up and stealing focus. The rule is simple: touch each email once. Respond, delegate, archive, or delete—then move on.

Batching beats bouncing. Rather than checking email all day like a nervous tic, set fixed times to process messages. Twice a day works for most leaders—once mid-morning and once late afternoon. Real-time replies should be rare, not routine.

Clear communication protocols reduce noise. Your team needs to know how and when to use email. If a quick answer is needed, pick up the phone or use messaging. If email's the right tool, it should include:

- A clear subject line
- Concise content: short and on-point
- A clearly defined action step

Auto-replies aren't just polite—they're policy setters. A simple "Here's when I check email" message can reset expectations across the board and protect time for focused work.

Email management isn't busywork—it's strategic hygiene. Cleaner inboxes lead to clearer minds. Systems matter. The more you standardize your process, the less energy you waste on digital clutter.

Structure invites progress. Assigning designated times to respond keeps your day from being derailed by distractions. It's not about being unavailable—it's about being intentional.

When expectations are clear, communication improves. Fewer assumptions. Less urgency theater. Better work. That's the win.

Inbox mastery is leadership maturity. When you stop reacting to every ding, you create space for the work that actually moves the needle.

CALIBRATION QUESTIONS

1. How often do you check your email each day, and how does that impact your ability to focus on strategic work?
   → *Reveals patterns of reactivity and the hidden cost of interruption.*

2. What boundaries do you currently have around email— and where are they breaking down?
   → *Encourages awareness of weak spots in digital discipline.*

3. What percentage of your emails truly require your attention, and how many could be delegated, delayed, or deleted?
   → *Invites clarity around responsibility, efficiency, and control.*

4. How would your day change if you only checked email at two set times?
   → *Prompts consideration of batching and intentional scheduling.*

5. What tasks or conversations have suffered because your attention was divided?
   → *Invites reflection on real-world consequences of multitasking.*

6. What assumptions are you making about others' expectations for your response time?
   → *Challenges the pressure of immediacy and opens space for boundary-setting.*

7. What single system, script, or standard could reduce your email stress this week?
→ *Encourages low-bar, high-impact action toward healthier inbox habits.*

"Your inbox is loud. Your priorities should be louder."

RECOMMENDED RESOURCES

1. **World Without Email: Reimagining Work in an Age of Communication Overload** by Cal Newport
   This book directly addresses the communication chaos explored in Chapter 3. Newport challenges the hyperactive hive mind of modern workplaces and offers a roadmap for reducing email dependence. It reinforces the idea that email overload is not a necessary evil but a solvable problem, making it an ideal next read for leaders ready to build healthier communication systems.

2. **Deep Work: Rules for Focused Success in a Distracted World**
   by Cal Newport
   Chapter 3 emphasizes the value of uninterrupted focus—this book is a masterclass in cultivating it. Newport provides strategies for minimizing distractions like email and maximizing concentration. It aligns perfectly with the chapter's call to protect time for strategic, high-impact work.

3. **Essentialism: The Disciplined Pursuit of Less** by Greg McKeown
   This book supports the idea that not all emails—and not all tasks—are created equal. McKeown's philosophy of doing less, but better, reinforces the importance of structured communication and filtering distractions in service of meaningful productivity.

4. **Getting Things Done: The Art of Stress-Free Productivity** by David Allen Allen's system offers practical tools for processing information, including email, in a

way that reduces stress and improves clarity. Chapter 3's discussion on inbox zero and decision-making efficiency finds a natural extension in Allen's GTD framework.

5. **Indistractable: How to Control Your Attention and Choose Your Life** by Nir Eyal
If Chapter 3 left readers aware of how easily attention is hijacked by email, Eyal takes it a step further by teaching how to stay focused in an age of constant interruption. His tactics help reinforce boundaries and build internal discipline against distractions.

6. **The Four-Hour Workweek** by Timothy Ferriss
Ferriss's emphasis on automation, delegation, and eliminating unnecessary communication aligns with the idea of reducing time spent in the inbox. His unconventional productivity tips challenge traditional notions of busyness and offer bold alternatives to constant email checking.

7. **The Effective Executive: The Definitive Guide to Getting the Right Things Done** by Peter F. Drucker
Drucker's classic reminds leaders that effectiveness, not efficiency, is the highest goal. His insights on time management and prioritization bolster the chapter's message that reactive email habits undermine strategic leadership.

8. **The 4 Disciplines of Execution: Achieving Your Wildly Important Goals** by Chris McChesney, Sean Covey, and Jim Huling
This book provides a framework for focusing on top priorities in the face of daily distractions—like email. It pairs well with the chapter's call to protect focus time and set boundaries for communication chaos.

9. **Rework** by Jason Fried and David Heinemeier Hansson
   With a strong bias toward simplicity and clarity, Rework challenges traditional workplace norms—including the assumption that fast email response equals productivity. It encourages leaders to rethink the way work gets done and supports less reactive, more intentional habits.

10. **Measure What Matters: How Google, Bono, and the Gates Foundation Rock the World with OKRs** by John Doerr
    While not email-specific, this book focuses on aligning goals and measuring progress—making it easier to see which communications truly matter. For leaders working to reduce email overload, OKRs offer a structured lens to filter the noise and focus on what drives real results.

4 | PROCRASTINATION AND DECISION FATIGUE

"YOU CANNOT ESCAPE THE RESPONSIBILITY OF TOMORROW BY EVADING IT TODAY."

- ABRAHAM LINCOLN -

16th President of the United States

THE ROOT CAUSES OF PROCRASTINATION

I see you there—staring at the screen, fully aware of what needs doing, yet motionless. The call goes unmade. The project sits untouched. You promise yourself there's still time. But when "later" finally shows up, the task is still looming... and now it's dragging your peace of mind down with it.

This isn't laziness. It's not incompetence. It's something subtler—something that hijacks progress before we've even begun.

Procrastination often wears a disguise. Sometimes it's fear—fear of making the wrong move. Other times, it's a fog of unclear priorities, or simply too much coming at you all at once. Perfectionism plays its part too. You want the task done right—so you hesitate, knowing it'll take more time than you're ready to spend. And then there's avoidance: when a difficult task stares you down and retreat feels like the easier option. But avoidance doesn't delete the task—it just crams it into your mental junk drawer, where it hums in the background, draining energy.

And while we're here, let's not ignore wiring. Your temperament matters. If you're wired to seek harmony (hello, to my fellow Enneagram Nines), avoid conflict (high S in DISC), or emotionally absorb every task's weight (looking at you, high EQ empaths), the emotional load of a decision can be heavier than the task itself. Your style isn't wrong—it just needs a strategy.

Blame your brain, too. It's designed to conserve energy and seek comfort. It will gladly convince you that scrolling through emails is as good as replying to them. That researching a task counts as making progress. And if all else fails, it'll whisper the oldest lie in the book: "You'll have a fresh start tomorrow." Before long, you're not just kicking the can—you're building a mountain out of molehills, until the smallest task becomes a runaway snowball.

> *Procrastination is a clever thief—it robs us in small increments until the vault is empty.*

Here's the good news: breaking this pattern doesn't require a life overhaul. Like most meaningful change, it begins with small, steady steps. Tiny choices, consistently made, that begin to unravel the grip of procrastination—and return your time to its rightful owner: you.

WHY DECISION FATIGUE DRAINS TIME AND MENTAL ENERGY

From the moment your feet hit the floor, the choices begin. What should I wear? What should I eat? Which voicemail deserves my attention first? Do I tackle that meeting prep now or later? These decisions seem small—but like a slow drip from a leaky faucet, they quietly drain your cognitive reservoir.

By mid-afternoon, the effects start to show. Priorities blur. Mental focus frays. And by evening, even a simple question like "What's for dinner?" can feel like scaling a mountain in dress shoes.

This is decision fatigue—the slow erosion of your ability to choose well, caused by the sheer volume of decisions you make from sunrise to sundown. Early in the day, choosing feels easy. But as mental fuel burns off, your brain begins to conserve energy by either avoiding decisions, defaulting to impulsivity, or kicking-the-can entirely.

Decision fatigue isn't just a personal nuisance—it's a professional liability, especially for those in high-stakes leadership roles.

A study from Columbia University estimated that the average person makes about 70 decisions per day, but for CEOs and business owners, that number can soar into the hundreds. According to research published in the Harvard Business Review, senior leaders often spend more than 50% of their time making decisions, with many reporting a steep drop in decision quality as the day progresses. Another study by McKinsey found that 72% of executives felt burdened by the sheer volume of decisions required of them, leading to delays, delegation breakdowns, or defaulting to inaction.

This cognitive overload not only slows strategic momentum—it also erodes confidence. Leaders who were once decisive begin second-guessing themselves, and the ripple effects can stall entire teams. The irony? Many of these decisions aren't monumental—but they accumulate, exhaust, and ultimately distract from the ones that are.

Too often, the decisions that matter most are made only when pressure forces your hand.

Here's the trap: the brain doesn't differentiate between a decision about socks and a decision about strategy. Every choice costs something. And without boundaries or structure, your best thinking gets rationed to the wrong things at the wrong time.

All leaders make decisions—great leaders protect their energy for the right ones.

> *The goal isn't to eliminate resistance—*
> *it's to recognize it and move anyway.*

FOCUS FRAMES AND DECISION-MAKING SYSTEMS

Decisions never stop—but the burden of having to make them can get lighter.

One of the simplest ways to cut through overthinking is to use what I call a Focus Frame©: a short, defined window where you give a decision your full attention and nothing else. Instead of leaving the task open-ended or waiting for the mythical "right moment," you assign it a boundary. A start. A stop. A clean frame.

It works like this:

- Pick one decision that's been dragging on.
- Estimate how long it should reasonably take—then set a timer.
- During that time, no interruptions. No circling back. You're in the frame.
- When time's up, you stop, debrief, and determine the next move.

Let's say you've been avoiding your inbox. Set a 10-minute Focus Frame© and process as many messages as you can. Hiring decision looming? Frame 30 minutes to review the top resumes, make comparisons, and move one step closer to resolution.

If you unable to make a decision on a particular item during your Focus Frame, stop. Set another time slot to revisit and begin again.
The point isn't perfection—it's progress. Focus Frames help you bypass the mental stall-outs that cost time and momentum.

With practice, they become a reliable tool in the battle against decision fatigue.

Another effective approach is the two-minute rule: If a task takes less than two minutes, do it immediately. This clears out small decisions, freeing mental bandwidth for bigger ones.

One tool worth mentioning—if only briefly—is the Eisenhower Matrix, a timeless framework for sorting tasks by urgency and importance. At its core, it helps you separate what demands your attention from what simply demands your time. The Eisenhower Matrix has four quadrants:

Important and Urgent
Important but Not Urgent
Not Important but Urgent
Not Important and Not Urgent

1. Important \ Urgent	2. Important \ Not Urgent

3. Not Important \ Urgent	4. Not Important \ Not Urgent

This simple grid can reveal which decisions deserve action, which can be scheduled, which should be delegated, and which can be ignored altogether. If decision fatigue stems from treating everything like it matters equally, this matrix reminds you: it doesn't.

BUILDING MOMENTUM, ONE DECISION AT A TIME

Procrastination and decision fatigue aren't conquered in a day. They're worn down by rhythm—by small, repeated actions that build confidence, clarity, and control. Progress doesn't begin with tackling the biggest thing on your list; it begins with doing something. Even five minutes of focused action is often enough to break the inertia.

Start small. Pick one task you've been avoiding, set a timer for five minutes, and give it your full attention—no distractions, no switching tabs, no mental side quests, notifications on silent. When the timer goes off, stop. That's it. If it feels too easy, good. The goal here is momentum, not mastery.

Still stuck? Write down three tasks you've been putting off. Then pick the first one and commit to just ten minutes. The point is to reclaim agency.

Procrastination loses power
when you start moving.

Of course, the environment around you matters, too. Distractions are everywhere—and your brain is all too willing to welcome them. Every ping, ding, and pop-up promises quick relief from the discomfort of doing hard things. But the relief they offer is a lie. It breaks your focus and steals your rhythm.

If you're not sure how bad it's gotten, here's a simple test: Ask the people closest to you if they ever feel like they're competing with your phone for your undivided attention. Their answer might sting—but it could also be the wake-up call you need. If your device distracts you when you're with others, it's almost certainly sabotaging you when you're alone with your work.

Take control. Silence notifications when you enter a Focus Frame or begin a task that matters. Yes, you may feel some anxiety—What if there's an emergency? But let's be honest: when was the last time that actually happened? And if it did, wouldn't there be better systems in place than a banner alert on your lock screen?

Building better systems now will pay dividends for years to come. Set default decisions for common situations to reduce the number of choices you have to make. Automate what you can. Delegate where it makes sense. Use checklists to reduce mental load on repetitive tasks. Tackle decision-heavy work in the morning, when your energy levels are highest.

> *Most of us don't need more time;*
> *we need more traction.*

Try setting a daily 15-minute window—a kind of "rapid decision sprint"—to clear your backlog of simple choices. No overthinking. Just clarity, action, and forward motion.

End each week with a brief reflection:

- Where did decision fatigue creep in?
- What tasks or systems slowed you down?
- What worked—and what needs to be adjusted?

To put this into action, email **support@timegambitbook. com** with **"Toolbox Access"** in the subject line, and you'll receive the **Focus Frame Template**—along with the entire **Time Gambit Toolbox**, a growing collection of proven time-mastery tools and guides that we use with our clients.

CALIBRATION QUESTIONS

1. What kinds of tasks tend to linger on your to-do list the longest, and what stories do you tell yourself about why they can wait?
   → *Reveals patterns of delay and uncovers mental scripts that justify procrastination.*

2. When do you notice your ability to make decisions start to slip during the day—and what's usually happening around that time?
   → *Invites awareness of daily energy rhythms and situational triggers for decision fatigue.*

3. How do you typically respond when a task feels emotionally uncomfortable, unclear, or overwhelming?
   → *Highlights default avoidance behaviors and internal resistance.*

4. Which low-stakes decisions are stealing your focus from high-impact work?
   → *Encourages identification of mental clutter and low-return choices.*

5. What tasks or conversations have suffered because your attention was divided?
   → *Invites reflection on real-world consequences of multitasking.*

6. Where in your current workflow could a simple system or rule remove a recurring decision from your plate?
   → *Promotes systemization and default decision-setting as solutions to mental overload.*

7. What's one area of your work or life where "done" would serve you better than "perfect"?
   → *Exposes the perfectionism–procrastination link and invites a shift in mindset.*

> *If you're waiting for the perfect time to act, just know— procrastination has already called dibs on your schedule.*

FINAL THOUGHTS

A word for the perfectionists among us: ***Done is better than perfect***—especially for 99% of the decisions you make every day. Drive toward perfection only for the few things that truly matter. For everything else? Decide, then "move to the next play."

In the end, you don't need more time, you need fewer wasted decisions. Procrastination and decision fatigue thrive in chaos. Frameworks create freedom. The more you systematize your choices, the more control you reclaim over your time. So start small. Start intentionally. And keep moving—one decision at a time.

RECOMMENDED RESOURCES

1. **The Procrastination Equation: How to Stop Putting Things Off and Start Getting Stuff Done** by Dr. Piers Steel
   One of the most research-heavy explorations of procrastination, Steel's book breaks down the psychological forces behind delay—fear, impulsivity, low expectancy—and offers actionable ways to retrain your thinking. It deepens the science behind why we stall and supports the chapter's invitation to take small, deliberate steps toward momentum.

2. **The End of Procrastination** by Petr Ludwig
   This book bridges cognitive science with practical application, helping readers build discipline through structure and focus. Ludwig's emphasis on clarity of purpose and systematic habits reinforces the chapter's use of Focus Frames and decision-sorting frameworks like the Eisenhower Matrix.

3. **The Science of Overcoming Procrastination** by Patrick King
   King dives into the internal resistance patterns that feed procrastination—emotional friction, perfectionism, and fear of discomfort. It complements the chapter's message that avoidance is not laziness but often an unspoken emotional coping mechanism. His tools are direct, relatable, and actionable.

4. **The Art of Procrastination** by John Perry
   This clever and candid read offers a reframe: what if you could strategically procrastinate? Perry's concept of

"structured procrastination" might not match the Focus Frame's intensity, but it provides a humorous, philosophical take on how to redirect avoidance tendencies toward productive ends.

5. **Time is Money: A Guide to Effective Time Management for Entrepreneurs** by John Hall
   With an emphasis on entrepreneurs and decision-heavy roles, this book supports the chapter's focus on how cognitive overload derails leaders. Hall provides practical tips on how to simplify, systematize, and preserve mental bandwidth for what matters most.

6. **14 Essential Time Management Tips for Serious Entrepreneurs by** The Entrepreneur Journey
   A concise, tactical resource that echoes the chapter's structure-based mindset. This quick-hit guide reinforces the value of systems like default decisions, checklists, and blocking time for mental focus.

7. **Time Management for Entrepreneurs – 7 Effective Strategies** by Adapting Social
   This short and strategic guide aligns well with the chapter's call to eliminate unnecessary choices and delegate wherever possible. It's perfect for readers who want fast implementation without fluff.

5 | FIRE FIGHTING VS. PROACTIVE LEADERSHIP

"FIREFIGHTING IS FOR THE FIRE DEPARTMENT. LEADERS BUILD FIREPROOF SYSTEMS."

– CRAIG GROESCHEL –

American Author and Speaker

SMOKE IN THE CONTROL ROOM

The call came in before Zach even took his first sip of coffee. A client was livid—something about a shipment gone sideways. Before he could respond, his inbox chimed with a red-flag email. Then came the knock. Three team members, each with their own version of "urgent", stood outside his office like a delegation of dread. By 9:00 a.m., events had already foreshadowed his day.

"It's not supposed to be like this", Zach thought.

He had started the business 12 years ago with vision and grit. But lately, every day was little more than a fire-drill. One crisis resolved, another ready to take its place. Strategy? There was no time for strategy lately. His calendar was full, his desk a mess, and his mind scattered.

Where he once was leading, Zach was now reacting. The

five years prior, the company had scaled rapidly, but over the past 12 months things had plateaued. They weren't growing anymore and it started to feel like they were gasping for air.

Today was another one of those days when the clock struck five, he wasn't just tired, he was completely drained. It was that hollow kind of exhaustion where you know you were busy all day but can't point to a single thing that really mattered.

There was no more ignoring the pattern: The urgent was devouring the important.

Zach wasn't running the business anymore. The business was running him—and it wasn't being nice about it.

He began to notice the ripple effects. His team had stopped thinking for themselves. They'd grown dependent on his decisions, waiting for him to solve every bottleneck and untangle every mess. Delegation had stalled and confidence had reached an all-time low. No one wanted to take ownership if the boss was going to come to the rescue anyway.

And the worst part? He couldn't even blame them.

Things got real when he came to acknowledge that this is how he's been training them—unintentionally, of course—but training them nonetheless. They were trained to react instead of anticipate– to escalate instead of solve.

This wasn't leadership. It was survival with a title.

Reactive leadership is a treadmill with no off switch. It keeps you in motion, but never in momentum. Every decision feels rushed. Every win is short-lived. There's no building—only bailing.

Proactive leadership, on the other hand, is what Zach longed for. Not perfection, but progress. Not more hours, but more productive ones. He wanted to see around corners, not just survive collisions. To move from a firefighter's stance to a chess player's posture—thoughtful, deliberate, strategic.

FROM TRIAGE TO TRACTION

Things didn't change overnight.

There wasn't a single eureka moment. No mountaintop revelation. Just a quiet, frustrating Tuesday when Zach found himself staring blankly at his computer screen, trying to remember what he was supposed to be doing before the last fire broke out.

That was the moment he finally admitted: This isn't sustainable.

The business had grown. The team had expanded. But the systems hadn't. Processes that worked when it was just him and two others were now cracking under the weight of complexity. Without clear workflows or communication rhythms, every little hiccup turned into a full-blown emergency.

And the emergencies always found their way to him.

So Zach made a choice—not to overhaul everything at once, but to start with one stubborn question:

"What's the one fire I keep putting out that shouldn't even be mine?"

That question led to a second: "Why is it still mine?"

He started small. Instead of responding to every team issue in real time, he blocked a standing slot on his calendar: Daily Leadership Huddle—15 minutes, no more. If a problem could wait until then, it wasn't a crisis—it was just noise. That simple boundary exposed a deeper issue: no one knew who owned what.

So Zach worked with his team to create clarity. Every role got revisited; every responsibility mapped. He wasn't trying to micromanage—he was trying to untangle a web of invisible assumptions that had formed over years. Turned out, most of the fires weren't caused by incompetence... just confusion.

Next came the "decision bottleneck."

Zach realized that he was still the answer key for nearly every meaningful decision. Not because he wanted control, but because he had never built the systems or trust to let go. It wasn't enough to say "delegate more"—he had to build guardrails so others could take the wheel without running the business into a ditch.

So he started documenting. Slowly. One SOP (standard operating procedure) at a time.

The first was around client handoffs, which had become a recurring hotspot. The next tackled inbound requests from operations. Each system removed one more reason for someone to knock on his door with another "quick question."

Momentum followed clarity. The more Zach empowered others, the more he noticed something unexpected—his team got better. They stepped up. They made sharper calls. They even started spotting patterns he'd missed.

It wasn't magic. It was margin.

And that margin gave Zach something he hadn't had in months: space to think.

> *Time isn't lost all at once. It's traded away, piece by piece, to things that don't move the mission.*

That's when strategy returned. Not in a four-day offsite retreat, but in pockets of quiet—those early morning hours before the inbox erupted, or on afternoon walks when he could finally see the business from above, not just inside it.

He wasn't out of the weeds entirely, but the brush was clearing. Fires still happened, but they were rarer... and they weren't his to fight alone anymore.

Zach had traded chaos for traction.

Not because he worked harder—but because he started working on the right things.

YOU'RE NOT ALONE

Zach's story might sound familiar—and that's because it is.

Having coached executives and owners in this exact situation for over 15 years, I can tell you—Zach's experience isn't unusual. It's a predictable stage in the life-cycle of nearly every growing business. What starts as nimble and hands-on eventually becomes scattered and overwhelming, leaving many leaders buried by the very thing they built.

They're not lazy. They're not broken. They're just stuck in the inevitable friction between growth and infrastructure.

According to a report by the U.S. Chamber of Commerce, 60% of small business owners say they feel regularly overwhelmed by day-to-day operations, with a majority citing "time management" and "delegation" as their biggest ongoing challenges.

A Harvard Business Review study found that leaders of growing companies spend up to 80% of their time reacting to problems—not because they want to, but because the systems they need don't exist in their organization yet. Instead of leading the business, they're pulled into solving problems their team should be equipped to handle.

And here's another kicker: According to McKinsey, only 20% of a typical leader's time is spent on strategic work. The other 80%? Meetings, firefighting, micromanagement, and unstructured communication loops.

If that feels uncomfortably accurate… you're not alone. You're not failing. You're just under-system'd.

The good news? This doesn't need to be a permanent condition because it's a solvable one. The transition from reactive to proactive leadership doesn't require a full reinvention. It begins by recognizing the pattern—and reclaiming your role not as the Chief Problem Solver, but as the Chief Architect of how work gets done.

In the next section, I'll give you some ideas on how to turn it around.

THE PROACTIVE PIVOT

Proactive leadership isn't about having fewer problems—it's about having better ones. When you lead proactively, you stop being the firefighter and start being the architect. Instead of fixing a broken door, you figure out how to build a better one. You anticipate. You design. You allocate time and responsibility before the crisis shows up at your door. Here are five proven strategies that help leaders shift from reactive chaos to proactive clarity:

1. **Schedule Thinking Time, Not Just Doing Time**
   Most calendars are crammed with meetings and tasks—but rarely space for strategy. Proactive leaders passionately protect thinking time like it's a high-stakes meeting. Whether it's 30 minutes each morning or two hours every Friday, this space allows you to zoom out, spot patterns, and make decisions that shape the next chapter—not just survive the current one.

2. **Make Invisible Workflows Visible**
   Most fires start because someone assumed someone else was handling it. Document the recurring workflows in your business—client onboarding, inventory restocking, employee reviews, content publishing, whatever your world includes. You don't need a 30-page manual. Just a shared, accessible set of steps and roles that clarify who owns what, by when.

3. **Create a Triage System for Problems**
   Not every issue deserves your immediate attention. Create simple filters:
   - Is this urgent or just loud?
   - Is this mine or someone else's?
   - Does this need a response or a system?

   Leaders who triage well don't ignore problems—they route them to the right level and right time. That's maturity, not avoidance.

4. **Empower With Guardrails, Not Just Goals**
   Telling your team to "step up" without giving them clarity is like sending someone to the kitchen and saying, "Make dinner!" When you don't get what you expected, you can't blame the cook. Define clear decision rights:
   - What can they decide without you?
   - What should they escalate?

   When expectations are clear, ownership grows– and the constant back-and-forth slows. This is also where solid leadership talent will reveal itself among your team.

5. **Shift From Hero to Coach**
   In reactive cultures, the leader is the hero—rushing in to solve everything. But in proactive cultures, the leader becomes the coach—developing others to solve problems on their own. Ask more questions. Give fewer answers. Challenge your team to bring solutions, not just issues.

These shifts don't happen overnight. But they compound— like interest in a healthy organization. One system clarified, one calendar block protected, one decision delegated—that's how leaders move from exhaustion to momentum.

The way I see it:

> *You can spend your energy putting out fires— or building something that doesn't burn.*

CALIBRATION QUESTIONS

1. Where in your leadership are you most often reacting instead of anticipating?
   → *Helps uncover blind spots where fire-fighting has become the norm.*

2. What systems (or lack thereof) are contributing to repeated interruptions or breakdowns?
   → *Invites reflection on how operational gaps fuel reactivity.*

3. In what areas have you accepted chaos as "just the way it is"?
   → *Challenges the leader to identify where resignation has replaced intentionality.*

4. Who regularly brings you problems they should be solving themselves—and why?
   → *Exposes unclear delegation, authority gaps, or learned dependency.*

5. What would it take to design a week where strategy gets your best time, not your leftover time?
→ *Prompts the leader to imagine a proactively structured schedule.*

6. Where are you too accessible—and what's the cost of that availability?
→ *Helps assess the impact of leader-centric bottlenecks and boundary erosion.*

If these questions feel uncomfortable, good. That means they're getting close to something that matters.

FINAL THOUGHTS

The truth is, firefighting feels noble in the moment. You swoop in, save the day, and everyone looks to you as the hero. But the long-term cost is steep—burnout, stalled growth, and a team that never matures beyond dependency.

Proactive leadership takes a different kind of courage. It requires slowing down long enough to ask the harder questions, to build the systems that don't yet exist, and to trust others with responsibility you've been carrying alone. It's less about brilliance in the moment and more about discipline over time.

If you see yourself in Zach's story, you're not broken—you're just overdue for a pivot. Every leader reaches this crossroad. The ones who move forward choose to exchange urgency for intentionality, chaos for clarity, and heroics for coaching.

When it all shakes out, leadership isn't about how many fires you put out. It's about how well you design an environment where fires don't spread in the first place. That's the shift from survival to stewardship. And that shift is where real momentum begins.

RECOMMENDED RESOURCES

1. **The 7 Habits of Highly Effective People** by Stephen R. Covey
Covey's foundational work is a masterclass in proactive living. His principles—like "be proactive," "begin with the end in mind," and "put first things first"—speak directly to leaders who need to reclaim their role from daily chaos and redesign their leadership rhythm.

2. **Essentialism: The Disciplined Pursuit of Less** by Greg McKeown
This book reframes productivity around clarity and purpose. For reactive leaders drowning in tasks, McKeown offers a roadmap to simplify, focus, and eliminate the nonessential—freeing space for the kind of high-impact work that leadership requires.

3. **The One Thing** by Gary Keller and Jay Papasan
Keller and Papasan argue that success isn't about doing everything—it's about doing the right thing. Their focus-based framework complements the proactive leader's shift toward intentionality and long-term traction, not just daily motion.

4. **Deep Work: Rules for Focused Success in a Distracted World** by Cal Newport
Newport champions the value of undistracted time and mental clarity. His approach underscores the importance of protecting strategic thinking time—one of the first disciplines a reactive leader must reclaim on the journey to proactivity.

5. **High Output Management** by Andrew S. Grove
   This classic on operations and delegation provides real-world tactics for turning leadership energy into scalable systems. Grove's insights reinforce the message that great leaders don't fix everything—they build frameworks that make great work possible.

6. **The Effective Executive** by Peter F. Drucker
   Drucker's timeless principles on time, decision-making, and contribution remind leaders that busyness isn't the goal—effectiveness is. His work validates the need to shift from reactive tasks to intentional, results-oriented leadership.

7. **Atomic Habits** by James Clear
   Clear offers practical wisdom for building new habits that stick—ideal for leaders trying to replace reactive tendencies with proactive routines. His message reinforces the idea that transformation happens through small, repeated changes.

   Getting Things Done: The Art of Stress-Free Productivity by David Allen Allen's system helps leaders regain control of their time and mental bandwidth. It pairs naturally with the chapter's call to reclaim focus, reduce overwhelm, and prevent emergencies before they erupt.

8. **Leadership and Self-Deception** by The Arbinger Institute
   This deeper dive into mindset challenges leaders to examine how their own blind spots contribute to the chaos they experience. It's a fitting companion for readers ready to confront the personal roots of reactive leadership and step into something more effective.

9. **Multipliers: How the Best Leaders Make Everyone Smarter** by Liz Wiseman
   Wiseman explores how great leaders create environments where people thrive, take ownership, and solve problems without micromanagement. This aligns perfectly with the chapter's theme of shifting from reactive heroism to proactive leadership by empowering others and building systems that scale beyond the leader.

TIME GAMBIT

6 | PERFECTIONISM PARALYSIS

"A GOOD PLAN VIOLENTLY EXECUTED NOW IS
BETTER THAN A PERFECT PLAN
EXECUTED NEXT WEEK."

- GEORGE S. PATTON -

General, United States Army

WHEN GOOD ENOUGH IS BETTER THAN PERFECT

I have a good friend—someone I've known for many years—who has always had an entrepreneurial spirit. Creativity has never been his problem. He's constantly brimming with ideas that could genuinely bring value to the world.

Throughout his career, he worked against the backdrop of ambitious projects, always chasing the next big idea. One particular endeavor stands out in my memory. It was a website—his passion project—the embodiment of months of effort, meticulous planning, and a relentless pursuit of excellence.

The first time I saw it, I was blown away. The design, the attention to detail, the user experience—it was all incredibly well-thought-out. Before apps made it easy to generate visual content, he was hiring artists to create custom illustrations, ensuring his site had a unique and polished aesthetic.

He spent months refining it, frequently asking me to review his progress and provide feedback. I always enjoyed these reviews, and each time, I was amazed by the quality of his work. His vision was clear, and the execution was impressive.

But then, something strange happened.

After countless hours of development, he became dissatisfied. The WordPress template he had chosen—one that he had stretched to its absolute limits—was now holding him back. There were design elements and functionalities he couldn't quite achieve, and that frustration started to eat at him.

One day, he reached out for another review. But when I pulled up the website, I was stunned.

Though equally beautiful, it looked nothing like what I had seen before.

Everything was different—the layout, the visuals, the user flow. It was as if he had scrapped months of hard work and started over from scratch. And, in fact, that's exactly what had happened.

When I asked why he had made such a drastic change, he explained his frustration. The original design, despite all the work and refinement, no longer felt fresh to him. It felt stale—but only to him. The world had never even seen it.

He was caught in a cycle of relentless tweaking, redesigning, and perfecting—so much so that he never actually launched the website. He never allowed his work to be experienced by the audience he had built it for.

This was the first, and without question the most dramatic, case of perfectionism paralysis that I had ever encountered. But over the years, I've seen it happen again and again—whether with entrepreneurs, creatives, or business leaders.

> *Perfection doesn't propel when it paralyzes.*

We assume that because we've spent countless hours refining our work, everyone else will experience it with the same level of scrutiny. But they won't. In a first-time encounter, small imperfections are irrelevant. To a customer, function matters far more than flawlessness.

Anyone in my orbit has heard me say (ad nauseam), "Done is better than perfect." Not because I believe in putting subpar work into the world, but because waiting for perfection too often translates to missed opportunities.

Think about it—Toyota didn't wait until they had the perfect car before rolling their first model off the production line. If they had, they never would have become the global powerhouse they are today. Instead, they followed a system of continuous improvement. The first version was good enough, and each iteration became better over time. What's more, in the case of Toyota's influence on industry, the rest of the manufacturing world would have denied the immeasurable benefit of systems like TPS (Toyota Production System) and LEAN Manufacturing.

I've heard it said (and I agree) that waiting for the perfect moment is like waiting for rush-hour traffic to disappear before merging onto the highway—it's never going to happen. Businesses that hold back until every last detail is fine-tuned lose time, momentum, and potential customers. A near-perfect version in your hands today is worth far more than a flawless version stuck in development tomorrow. The market moves fast, and while you're polishing, someone else is "delivering."

Too many business owners fall into this trap. Your solution to someone else's need never feels quite polished enough. The product isn't "ready" yet. The marketing message could be tweaked just one more time. Sound familiar? The pursuit of perfection doesn't just slow things down—it can grind progress to a screeching halt.

Here's the gut punch: time spent obsessing over minor details rarely translates into success. Customers don't care if you spent an extra month adjusting a color palette; they care if your product works. They're looking for solutions, not a masterpiece of over-refinement. The businesses that move forward with "good enough" consistently outperform those chasing an unattainable ideal.

The most successful leaders understand this. They launch early, adapt quickly, and let real-world feedback shape the final product. They know that speed creates opportunity—because an imperfect product in the hands of customers is always better than a perfect one stuck in limbo.

PERFECTIONISM IS A SHAPE-SHIFTER

Perfectionism rarely shows up waving red flags—instead, it wears the mask of excellence. It poses as high standards, sharp attention to detail, or the noble desire to "get it right." But behind the scenes, it quietly stalls progress. If you recognize any of the patterns below, perfectionism might be holding more sway than you think:

- **Projects linger in limbo.** That website redesign? Still in progress. The marketing campaign? One more round of edits. The product launch? Just needs a little more polish. If this sounds familiar, perfectionism is stalling progress.
- **Decisions take forever.** If every choice turns into an hours-long debate with endless revisions, perfectionism is at play. Speed matters—delays cost more than minor imperfections ever will.
- **Deadlines are just suggestions.** If "launch day" keeps shifting forward because things aren't "quite there yet," you're letting perfectionism control the timeline. A deadline should be a commitment, not a moving target.
- **Minor details steal focus.** If you're spending more time adjusting a font size than refining your overall strategy, it's time for a priority check. Details matter, but they should never overshadow progress.
- **Delegation feels impossible.** Micromanaging every task because "no one does it quite like you" is a surefire way to slow things down. A great team can only move forward if you trust them to execute.

- **Fear masquerades as perfection.** Perfectionism and fear often go hand in hand. If you find yourself endlessly refining, ask yourself: Am I improving this, or am I just afraid of launching?
- **Customer needs take a backseat.** Sometimes, we perfect things our audience doesn't even want improved. Businesses thrive by listening to customers—not by chasing an internal vision of flawlessness.
- **Creativity gets stifled.** If every idea must be fully polished before it's shared, you'll never get new ones off the ground. Innovation happens in motion, not in hesitation.
- **Stress levels skyrocket.** Nothing is ever "good enough," leading to frustration, burnout, and exhaustion. The pursuit of perfect often drains more energy than it's worth.

> *The first step out of perfectionism isn't fixing more—it's releasing the need to.*

THE PRODUCT LAUNCH THAT TOOK FOREVER

Another associate of mine spent nearly two years fine-tuning her online course before launching. She re-recorded lessons, rewrote scripts, and edited videos to a very high standard. While she was polishing, competitors released their courses, built customer bases, and established themselves in the market.

By the time she finally launched, the landscape had changed. The demand wasn't the same. Her competitors had built brand loyalty while she was still tinkering behind the scenes. She had the most polished course—but a smaller audience was left to buy it.

Meanwhile, another business owner took the opposite approach. He launched an early version of his course, gathered feedback, and improved it along the way. Within a year, he had a loyal customer base, repeat buyers, and a reputation as a thought leader in his field. His course evolved based on real-world needs, not an imagined ideal.

These two stories expose a simple truth: Waiting for perfect isn't strategy—it's surrendering your place in line.

Embrace Progress Over Perfection

- **Action creates momentum.** Every step forward teaches something new. Even imperfect work gives you data. No movement? No feedback. No growth.
- **Deadlines should mean something.** Without a hard stop, perfectionism keeps shifting the finish line. Pick a launch date—and hold the line.
- **Perfection is a myth.** No project is flawless. Even the best brands iterate constantly. Deliver value now, improve later.
- **Customers—not you—define success.** They don't care how many times you polished it. They care whether it works. Ship it, listen, adjust.
- **Progress beats hesitation.** A project sitting in development gathers dust. One launched and tested evolves and improves. Execution creates success—not endless revisions.
- **Set limits on revisions.** If you don't decide when to stop tweaking, you never will. Cap the number of revisions—and move forward.
- **Trust your team.** Micromanaging every detail slows everything down. If you can't delegate, you can't scale.
- **Take calculated risks.** Perfectionism disguises itself as caution, but often, it's just fear. Growth comes from action—not waiting for certainty.

> *When it all shakes out, done is always*
> *better than perfect.*

CALIBRATION QUESTIONS

1. What has my perfectionism cost me—financially, emotionally, or mentally?
   → *Invites reflection on the hidden toll of always chasing flawless.*

2. What idea or project have I kept in limbo, waiting for the perfect moment?
   → *Encourages identification of opportunities delayed by over-refinement.*

3. Where do I obsess over details that don't actually move the needle?
→ *Prompts awareness of where energy is being misallocated.*

4. How often do I shift deadlines because something doesn't feel "just right"?
→ *Reveals perfectionism's influence on follow-through.*

5. When have I missed an opportunity because I waited too long to act?
→ *Pushes reflection on the real cost of hesitation.*

6. How comfortable am I with "good enough"—and where could I loosen my grip?

→ *Explores mindset around progress vs. perfection.*

7. What holds me back from delegating more—fear of mistakes, loss of control, or something else?

→ *Uncovers root resistance to sharing responsibility.*

*Progress doesn't come from getting it perfect—
it comes from getting it moving.*

RECOMMENDED RESOURCES

1. **The User Method: How Entrepreneurs Create Successful Innovations**
by Jeff Schwarting
This book explores how successful entrepreneurs launch early, observe user behavior, and iterate in real-time—often bypassing perfection in favor of relevance. Schwarting shows how innovation thrives through responsiveness, not over-engineering. It reinforces the chapter's core truth: progress guided by feedback beats delay driven by fear.

2. **The Lean Startup** by Eric Ries
This book is a practical guide to launching products quickly and learning through iteration. It reinforces the idea from this chapter that action creates momentum, and waiting for perfection only delays valuable feedback and growth.

3. **Essentialism: The Disciplined Pursuit of Less** by Greg McKeown
McKeown teaches you how to cut through the noise and focus on what truly matters. Readers who get stuck obsessing over minor details will find clarity and practical tools to escape perfectionist overcommitment.

4. **The 4-Hour Workweek** by Timothy Ferriss
Ferriss encourages readers to eliminate unnecessary work, delegate with confidence, and challenge conventional norms—perfect for those struggling to let go of control or battling the need to perfect every task themselves.

5. **Rework** by Jason Fried & David Heinemeier Hansson
Bold and refreshingly contrarian, this book shatters the

myth that you need to over-plan or over-perfect. Its bite-sized insights will energize readers to ship fast, adapt on the fly, and embrace simplicity over delay.

6. **The Gifts of Imperfection** by Brené Brown
A deeply human look at the roots of perfectionism, shame, and fear, this book encourages vulnerability and authenticity—an emotional counterpart to the action-focused mindset this chapter promotes.

7. **Progress Over Perfection: A Guide to Mindful Productivity** by Emma Norris
Norris champions the exact philosophy this chapter is built upon. Her advice helps readers reduce overwhelm, start messy, and build productive habits without being weighed down by unrealistic standards.

8. **Are You A Perfect Dam Leader?** by Barbara D'Anna
This book dives into perfectionism in leadership and offers strategies for overcoming it. A great choice for readers who recognized themselves in the leadership pitfalls outlined in this chapter and want actionable change.

9. **Overcoming Perfectionism** by Ann W. SmithA thoughtful exploration of the emotional patterns behind perfectionism. This resource is valuable for readers seeking to heal the internal drivers that keep them stuck in cycles of over-refinement and self-doubt.

10. **The Infinite Game** by Simon Sinek
Sinek's framework encourages long-term thinking, adaptability, and resilience over short-term perfection. For readers ready to reframe success as a journey of continuous growth, this book provides the strategic vision to match the chapter's practical insights.

7 | VISION AND CLARITY

"IF YOU DON'T KNOW WHERE YOU ARE GOING, YOU'LL END UP SOMEPLACE ELSE."

– YOGI BERRA –

19x All-Star Catcher, NY Yankees

WHERE VISION BLURS, TIME WANDERS

I recently worked with a business owner who had built his company from the ground up. Ambitious and driven, he poured long hours into his business—but never felt like he was gaining ground. "I start my day intending to get important things done," he admitted, "but by the end, I'm drained and haven't made real progress on what matters most."

So I asked a simple question: "What exactly are your priorities?"

The look on his face—and the long pause that followed—said it all.

If you don't know where you're going, how will you know when you've arrived? Or worse, how will you recognize when you've gone off course?

Your daily time usage is the clearest reflection of your respect for and understanding of your goals—or the absence of them. When goals are fuzzy or undefined, your time gets hijacked by reactivity. Instead of deliberate movement, you're pulled in every direction. Meetings fill the calendar. Emails and phone calls dictate your flow. The day ends with little to show but exhaustion and a vague sense of lost opportunity.

> *Unprioritized tasks that are mistakenly deemed urgent expand to fill the void, crowding out what truly matters.*

Running a business without clear goals is like managing an investment portfolio without a strategy. Resources get scattered. Returns are unpredictable. Every "quick" favor, low-impact meeting or unnecessary task becomes a withdrawal from your productivity account. Without defined goals, those withdrawals happen constantly—and usually without resistance.

The result? Time gets squandered. Progress doesn't get the payout.

Lack of clarity also undermines delegation. If you're not sure where you're headed, your team won't be either. They default to busywork or sit idle waiting for direction. When priorities shift daily, confusion and overwhelm replace momentum. Projects stall. Deadlines drift. Morale dips.

> *The highest-performing teams operate on clear, shared objectives—giving each task meaning and direction.*

Your calendar is a mirror. If it reflects a flood of meetings, emails, and low-value tasks, it's time to reassess. Are your real priorities showing up?

Time only behaves in your favor when it's given direction. Without clarity, it gets spent on what feels urgent rather than what's important.

> *Clarity breeds focus. Focus channels effort. And effort, when aimed well, produces results that matter.*

THE FOUNDATION OF CLARITY: VISION, PURPOSE, AND VALUES

Before we dive into the mechanics of setting goals, we need to lay the groundwork. True clarity doesn't begin with action—it begins with alignment. And that alignment is built on three anchors: Vision, Purpose, and Values.

> *Vision is what you see; Purpose is why it matters; Values are how you'll get there.*

Vision is the mental picture of the future you're working toward. It's the destination—the full expression of what success looks like for you. Without a defined vision, your efforts lack unifying direction. You may stay busy, but the impact remains scattered. Every meaningful goal should move you closer to that vision.

Purpose is the why behind your work. It answers the question: Why does this matter? Purpose adds meaning to vision, taking it beyond a dream, and serves as your decision-making compass. When purpose is present, goals gain significance— not just urgency. Without it, even well-executed strategies can feel hollow.

Values define how you operate. They are your non-negotiables—your internal code. Clear values provide boundaries and alignment. They shape organizational culture. They guide behavior. They ensure your goals stay true to who you are and what you stand for. When you operate outside your values, friction increases and momentum stalls. And often, businesses fail.

Now, to be clear—this chapter isn't about defining Vision, Purpose, and Values. That work belongs upstream. But these elements are the soil in which clarity grows. If you haven't clarified them yet, now's the time. Every strategy in this chapter works best when rooted in a firm foundation.

SETTING SMART GOALS AND WEEKLY REVIEWS

I once worked with a business owner who felt completely overwhelmed. Maybe you can relate. She was handling everything herself—constantly in motion, but making little meaningful progress.
I asked her to define her biggest goal. She said, "Grow the business." That's not a goal—it's a wish.

We turned that wish into something tangible: "Increase revenue by 20% over six months by acquiring 10 new high-ticket clients." Now she had something to measure, a direction to pursue.

We used a classic framework to do it: the SMART Goal system, introduced by George T. Doran back in 1981.

SMART Goals are:

1. **Specific:** You know exactly what needs to happen.
   Make sure you can answer the "W" questions: who, what, where, when, why. Who is involved? What do you want to accomplish? Where will this happen? Why do you want to do this or understand this? By being specific, you create a foundation to stay focused on your objective.

2. **Measurable:** You can track your progress.
   Make sure there is some way to measure your goal. How will you know when you have achieved your goal or when you have enough information to make a plan? These are the questions you need to ask. By having a specific way to measure success, you will know what you have achieved.

3. **Achievable:** It's within reach, not a fantasy.
   Are you fit for this? Do you have the skills necessary to reach your goals or to make your decision? Do you have the resources necessary and the time required? If not, you may need to reassess your goal. If it is unattainable, you will become frustrated and give up. By making sure you have the skills and resources necessary to attain your goal, you'll be able to keep the wheels rolling when the work gets more difficult.

4. **Relevant:** It aligns with your vision and values.
   Your values will be the compass that guides your actions and decisions. If your goals do not align with your values, you'll struggle to complete them.

5. **Time-bound:** There's a finish line that drives urgency.
   Every goal should be grounded in a time frame. If there is no sense of urgency, you will never complete it. Don't make the timeframe so short that it becomes impossible to achieve your goal in the given time. It should be a realistic but challenging time frame to keep it interesting.

When a goal checks all five boxes, it transforms from vague intent to actionable blueprint. Without those boundaries, goals become foggy hopes that fade with each passing week, and every setback or question becomes a puzzle that can't be solved.

But setting the goal is just the start. You also need to review it regularly—I recommend at least once a week. Without that rhythm, drift happens. You stop steering and start reacting.

MAKING IT WORK

Set aside 30 minutes at the end of each week to review:

1. What worked—and why? Each goal will have a different set of procedures.
2. What didn't—and why? Use the information you've gathered to understand what went wrong.
3. What needs to be recalibrated? Reason out a solution.
4. Did your time align with your stated priorities?
5. Where did distractions creep in?

This simple habit keeps your goals from fading into the background and helps you course-correct before a week turns into a wasted month.

Write your goals down—and keep them in your line of sight. On your desk. In your planner. On a wall. As a digital lock screen. A goal unseen is a goal forgotten.

Even better? Review them daily. Align each day's tasks with your larger objectives. And when a shiny new opportunity pops up, measure it against your goals. Will this move me closer—or pull me off course?

Success isn't about grinding harder. It's about working with greater precision. Most people don't fail for lack of effort— they fail for lack of clarity. Set SMART goals. Review them frequently. Align your time with your targets. That's how you build the future you actually want.

Distraction-proofing your calendar begins with commitment. If you allow minor tasks to seep into your schedule, they will. So, block off time for goal-focused work. Schedule it the same way you would a meeting—and treat it as non-negotiable. Your business depends on it.

> *When you know what you stand for,*
> *you waste less time chasing what doesn't align.*

To raise the stakes, share your goals with someone you trust. A friend, a coach, a mentor. Someone who will nudge you when you drift or settle for less than you're capable of. Others often see mission creep before we do.

Research backs this up. One study found that sharing your goals increases the likelihood of success to 65%. Add regular check-ins with a coach or accountability partner, and your chance of success jumps to 95%. The Association for Financial Counseling & Planning Education echoes this finding: when accountability is scheduled, failure rates drop to just 5%. That's the power of structured follow-through.

And don't forget—goals aren't set in stone. What serves you today may need tweaking next month. Markets shift. Needs change. A plan that once felt solid can become stale. Don't cling to it out of habit.

CALIBRATION QUESTIONS

1. When was the last time I clearly defined my top three business priorities?
   → *Encourages reflection on how recently I've aligned my focus areas.*

2. If someone analyzed my calendar from last week, what would they say my true priorities are?
→ *Reveals potential gaps between what I intended to prioritize and where my time actually went.*

3. How often do I end the day feeling like I made real progress on meaningful work?
→ *Surfaces the difference between staying busy and making genuine headway.*

4. Do my current goals follow the SMART framework, or are they still vague ambitions?
→ *Helps me evaluate whether my goals are clearly structured or just loosely defined.*

5. What distractions regularly pull me away from my high-value work?
→ *Invites reflection on the recurring culprits that derail my focus.*

6. How confident am I in my ability to delegate effectively and give clear direction to my team?
→ *Exposes whether I'm equipping others or holding too much myself.*

7. If I had to eliminate three low-value tasks from my schedule today, what would they be?
→ *Challenges me to identify time traps and reclaim capacity for what matters.*

Clarity doesn't come from thinking harder—
it comes from answering sharper questions.

FINAL THOUGHTS

How you spend your time should reflect the outcomes you're aiming for. Clarity and vision aren't optional—they're the foundation of effective leadership. Take control of your calendar before it takes control of you. Without a clear plan, success remains elusive.

The most effective business owners define their direction, prioritize with intention, and align daily use of time with long-term goals. When you commit to these principles, growth becomes measurable—not just in productivity, but in the strength and trajectory of your entire business.

RECOMMENDED RESOURCES

1. **Measure What Matters** by John Doerr
   This book introduces the OKR (Objectives and Key Results) framework, a practical complement to SMART goals. It reinforces the value of measurable clarity and strategic alignment, key themes of this chapter.

2. **The One Thing** by Gary Keller & Jay Papasan
   Focused on eliminating distraction and zeroing in on what matters most, this book echoes the chapter's core argument that clarity of focus fuels meaningful progress.

3. **Essentialism** by Greg McKeown
   Essentialism teaches the disciplined pursuit of less, encouraging leaders to eliminate non-essentials. It aligns perfectly with the emphasis on prioritization and intentionality in time usage.

4. **Atomic Habits** by James Clear
   This book connects deeply with the practical strategies in this chapter. It reinforces the power of small, measurable changes and the impact of habit-based systems that support clear goals.

5. **Your Best Year Ever** by Michael Hyatt
   Hyatt walks readers through a goal-setting framework that integrates mindset, motivation, and structure—an excellent parallel to SMART goals and the weekly review habit discussed in the chapter.

6. **The 12 Week Year** by Brian Moran & Michael Lennington
This high-performance productivity system redefines execution by focusing on short-term cycles to achieve long-term results. It pairs well with the chapter's ideas around goal focus, time blocking, and accountability.

7. **Deep Purpose** by Ranjay Gulati
A fantastic complement to the section on Vision, Purpose, and Values. This book explores how organizations can thrive by anchoring their strategy and culture in a deeper sense of purpose.

8. **The EntreLeadership Podcast** by Ramsey Solutions
This podcast features interviews with business leaders on topics ranging from leadership to goal setting. Several episodes touch on team alignment, delegation, and strategic clarity.

9. **Lead to Win** with Michael Hyatt & Megan Hyatt Miller
This podcast focuses on productivity, leadership, and vision—all central to this chapter. Episodes often include tools and real-life examples that help bring structure to goal setting.

10. **The Harvard Business Review – Management Tip of the Day**
(Email & Blog)
A brief, high-value resource that reinforces leadership clarity, time prioritization, and strategic alignment—useful for reinforcing weekly review habits.

11. **Working Backwards** by Colin Bryar & Bill Carr
A behind-the-scenes look at Amazon's strategy practices, this book shows how aligning goals with customer-centric vision and values drives long-term success.

12. The Clarity Journal by Becca Ribbing
This resource helps readers slow down and ask better questions, making it an ideal pairing with the chapter's calibration questions and emphasis on clarity through self-inquiry.

8 DISTRACTIONS IN A DIGITAL WORLD

"THERE ARE ALWAYS DISTRACTIONS, IF YOU ALLOW THEM."

- TONY LA RUSSA -
MLB Head Coach, Author

THE HIDDEN COST OF DIGITAL INTERRUPTIONS

As I sit down to write this, my phone lights up—my Notification Center lists one ping for an email, another for a Slack mention, and a third from an app I don't even remember installing. Sound familiar? These aren't just distractions— they're productivity assassins, each one pulling your focus just far enough off course to derail meaningful work.

I've spent years coaching high-performing leaders, and I've seen firsthand how devastating these digital micro-interruptions can be. The myth of multitasking still floats around, but here's the truth: the modern workplace is rigged for reactivity. And unless you're ruthlessly intentional, you'll spend your entire day responding instead of leading.

Take Sarah, for example—a sharp, capable CEO running a booming e-commerce brand. On a whim, she decided to audit her digital interruptions over the course of a week. The numbers floored her: 137 Slack notifications, 242 emails, and 89 texts. In just five days, nearly four hours per day had been swallowed up—not by projects or planning—but by pings.

And as we noted back in Chapter 3, a study out of UC Irvine revealed that after just one interruption, it takes an average of 23 minutes and 15 seconds to regain full focus. That stat becomes even more sobering when you realize how often leaders like Sarah are pulled off course—hour after hour, task after task.

Sarah is not an outlier. She's the norm. The daily toll of notifications, alerts, and status checks adds up to what I call death by a thousand digital cuts. And the worst part? Most leaders don't even realize it's happening—until their focus, momentum, and strategic edge have quietly eroded.

> *You can't out-hustle digital distraction—*
> *you have to outsmart it.*

THE COGNITIVE TOLL OF DISTRACTION

Here's the thing about focus—it's not instant. Your brain takes 15 to 25 minutes to enter a state of deep concentration. But every ping, buzz, or pop-up pulls you right back to the base of the hill, forcing your brain to push the boulder of attention uphill… again. And again. And again.

We touched on this in earlier chapters, but it bears repeating: distraction is not just a nuisance—it's a performance killer. Stanford research shows that frequent task-switching doesn't just waste time; it increases error rates by up to 50%. Imagine your team making twice as many mistakes—not because they lack skill, but because they can't protect their attention. That's not just inefficient. It's dangerous.

But the fallout goes beyond typos and missed details. Every time you're interrupted, your brain lights up to process the new input, burning cognitive fuel and accelerating mental fatigue. When this happens dozens of times a day, the result is decision fatigue—an invisible weight that quietly sabotages your ability to think clearly, prioritize well, and lead effectively.

And it doesn't stop at brainpower. There's an emotional toll, too. Micro-interruptions keep your nervous system in a constant state of alert. Cortisol, one of your body's key stress hormones, floods the system with every ding. Left unchecked, this creates a baseline of chronic tension—leading to irritability, anxiety, and that slow, grinding sense of depletion that turns otherwise brilliant leaders into reactive shells of themselves.

Sarah experienced this firsthand. Despite her intelligence and drive, she noticed a disturbing pattern: the more fragmented her attention became, the shallower her thinking turned. Strategic planning sessions felt rushed. Creative ideas came slower. Her once-clear vision grew foggy—not because she lacked ability, but because she couldn't buy herself a stretch of protected, focused time.

This is what most leaders miss: deep work requires uninterrupted space. Complex challenges demand 90-minute stretches of focused problem-solving. And yet, for many leaders, 40 minutes of silence feels like a luxury. I often compare it to reading a novel one sentence at a time over the course of a year. Sure, you may technically get through it—but you'll never grasp the story arc, the nuance, or the bigger picture that makes it worth reading in the first place.

> *You don't drown in one notification. You drown in the undertow of a hundred ignored refocuses.*

THE FOCUS TAX

The financial fallout of digital interruption isn't just theoretical—it's measurable. I recently consulted a tech company that had run the numbers and discovered notification-related losses totaled $380,000 annually for their 50-person team. That figure factored in time lost regaining focus, stress-related absences, and reduced work quality. And if you're thinking, "That sounds high," think again. That's just the visible cost.

The real damage runs deeper. Constant interruptions don't just siphon minutes—they rewire your brain. Every ping of your smartphone trains your neural pathways to prefer novelty over focus, distraction over depth. It's like feeding your brain fast food all day long—it might feel satisfying in the moment, but it's detrimental to your long-term health. And here's the plot twist: you're the one serving the plate.

YOUR SMARTPHONE IS SMARTER THAN YOU THINK

Smartphones revolutionized business—but they've also quietly become the most effective productivity saboteurs ever invented. In a recent analysis of 50 business owners, the average leader checked their phone 134 times per day. That's nearly 1,000 micro-interruptions each week, every one hijacking your cognitive flow.

The most shocking part? Most of those checks weren't necessary. One CEO in manufacturing discovered that 92% of his phone pickups were fueled by FOMO—not genuine business needs. His pattern wasn't strategic. It was compulsive.

The science backs this up. A University of Texas study found that just having your phone visible—not in use, just present— reduced participants' cognitive performance by 20% on complex tasks. That means simply glancing at your phone during a meeting makes you objectively dumber.

This isn't just about distraction—it's about addiction. Smartphone use triggers dopamine responses almost identical to those seen in gambling studies. These micro-doses of pleasure condition your brain to crave constant input... followed by a crash. Over time, your ability to engage in deep work erodes.

And the cost? Far beyond productivity. I've heard leaders confess to fractured attention in meetings, rising anxiety, and frayed relationships at home. Even so-called "quick checks" flood the nervous system with cortisol—your body's primary stress hormone—for two to three minutes per alert. At 134 interruptions a day, that's four to six hours of sustained stress. Daily.

> *Burnout doesn't break in—it's invited, every time you treat distraction like it's part of the job.*

DIGITAL DETOX: A STRATEGIC RESET

The goal isn't to ditch tech—it's to discipline it. I've led many business owners through digital detox programs, and the results speak for themselves:

1. 40% increase in productive output
2. 60% reduction in reported stress
3. Noticeable gains in clarity, decision-making, and team trust

The key? Strategic disconnection. You don't need to go off the grid. Think of it like cutting refined sugar—not all food.

Start with a notification audit. For 48 hours, log every alert you get. My clients typically discover that 80% of their notifications offer zero time-sensitive value. That data becomes your blueprint for a smarter digital strategy.

Then build physical boundaries. One company president I coached installed a "phone garage"—a simple charging station outside his office door. That one shift eliminated 67% of his daily distractions—without sacrificing availability for emergencies.

And don't forget the Time Vault StrategyTM (detailed shortly). One marketing agency CEO used this to create alert-free deep work windows for her team. Within weeks, project completion rates jumped 34%.

Small changes, big returns. The power lies in reclaiming your attention—not just for productivity's sake, but for your leadership legacy.

BUILDING SUSTAINABLE FOCUS HABITS

Focus isn't just a mindset—it's a system. If you want to lead with clarity in a world full of digital noise, you need more than good intentions. You need habits that are structured, trackable, and sustainable.

Over the years, I've introduced two key tools to business owners and executive teams to help them reclaim control over their time and attention: the Notification Audit and the Time Vault Strategy. Both are simple in design but powerful in practice. And both are included as downloadable templates at the end of this chapter.

Here's how to use them to build a life where focused work isn't the exception—it's the standard.

THE NOTIFICATION AUDIT: SPOT THE SILENT SABOTEURS

Before you can fix the distractions, you need to see them clearly. The Notification Audit is a diagnostic tool designed to help you identify which interruptions are stealing your time and which ones (if any) truly deserve your attention. Saved as a spreadsheet, collected data can be sorted by column later to reveal patterns. To receive the Notification Audit Template—and the rest of the Time Gambit Toolbox—simply email support@timegambitbook.com with "Toolbox Access" in the subject line.

Step 1: Track the Noise

For 48 hours, log every notification you receive—from email pings and Slack messages to text alerts and app nudges. Use the following fields:

- Date & Time – When the alert hit
- Source – Email, text, app, etc.
- Urgency (1–5) – Was it actually time-sensitive?
- Response Needed (Y/N) – Did you need to take action?
- Focus Disruption (1–5) – How much did it pull you off track?
- Action Taken – What you did in response
- Time to Refocus – How long it took to re-engage with your original task

Step 2: Spot the Patterns

Once you've collected the data, look for themes. Are most notifications non-urgent? Do certain apps or platforms generate the biggest disruptions? Are mornings worse than afternoons?

Step 3: Build a Smarter Strategy

Use your insights to adjust. Batch email replies. Silence texts during peak focus hours. Disable non-essential app alerts. Create rules that match the way you work best—not the way your smartphone wants you to.

Step 4: Reassess Regularly

Run the audit again in 30–60 days. Distractions evolve, and so should your strategy.

This isn't about digital abstinence—it's about digital alignment. When your tools serve your priorities, not the other way around, you win.

THE TIME VAULT STRATEGY: PROTECT YOUR DEEP WORK HOURS

High-level thinking doesn't happen by accident—it happens in protected space. The Time Vault Strategy helps you carve out uninterrupted blocks for your most important work, insulated from the noise of the day.

Step 1: Know Your Power Hours

Track your daily energy for a week. When are you mentally sharpest? Those are your prime hours—your "vault time."

Step 2: Set the Block

Pick a focus block length that works for you. Research supports 90-minute sessions, but anywhere from 60–120 minutes can be effective. Find your sweet spot.

Step 3: Prioritize the Right Work

Choose one high-impact task or strategic project for each

block. Write it down. Clarity before you begin is half the battle.

Step 4: Communicate Boundaries

Let your team know when you'll be offline. Set clear windows when you're available and off-limits. Most distractions are preventable with a little proactive communication.

Step 5: Define Emergencies

Only three categories warrant interruption during vault time:

- Health & Safety Threats
- Major Operational Failures
- Legal or Compliance Crises

Everything else? It can wait.

Step 6: Track What Matters

At the end of each session, measure success:

- What did you complete?
- How focused did you feel?
- What would you improve next time?

Step 7: Stay Accountable

Share your Time Vault plan with a coach or colleague. Let them check in weekly on your progress.

Step 8: Run Weekly Reviews

Each week, ask: Did I protect my vault time? Did I stay true to my boundaries? What small tweaks could make next week better?

When used consistently, the Time Vault becomes a leadership multiplier. It trains your brain, signals your priorities, and reclaims the mental real estate needed for your best work.

CALIBRATION QUESTIONS

1. How often do I let digital interruptions pull me out of deep work?
   → *Invites awareness of how frequently notifications disrupt strategic focus.*

2. What toll do these distractions take on the quality of my decisions?
   → *Prompts reflection on the ripple effect interruptions have on judgment and clarity.*

3. How have my unchecked notification habits shaped my emotional state—and my leadership?
   → *Encourages honest evaluation of the internal and external costs of distraction.*

4. What would a smarter, customized notification strategy look like for me?
   → *Use creative thinking around a personal approach to managing alerts.*

5. Are my "quick checks" really quick—or are they sabotaging my momentum?
   → *Challenges assumptions about harmless habits and their hidden time cost.*

6. What boundaries can I create between my tech tools and my best work?

→ *Leads to intentional action toward healthier digital limits.*

7. How will I track progress as I commit to a digital detox strategy?

→ *Encourages practical thinking around measurement, milestones, and success signals.*

Attention is your most valuable currency—spend it where it earns the highest return.

RECOMMENDED RESOURCES

1. **The Distracted Mind: Ancient Brains in a High-Tech World by Adam Gazzaley & Larry D. Rosen**
    This book explores the neuroscience behind why we struggle with focus in our tech-saturated lives. It aligns directly with the chapter's explanation of how notifications hijack our attention and deplete cognitive resources. Gazzaley and Rosen give readers a deeper scientific understanding of the battle between our evolutionary wiring and modern demands.

2. **Indistractable: How to Control Your Attention and Choose Your Life by Nir Eyal Eyal**
    offers a modern toolkit for resisting the pull of constant digital temptation. His concept of "traction versus distraction" dovetails nicely with the proactive boundaries discussed in this chapter. It reinforces the importance of intentional technology use, a theme central to the digital detox strategies described.

3. **Digital Minimalism: Choosing a Focused Life in a Noisy World by Cal Newport**
    Instead of repeating The Willpower Instinct, this follow-up from Newport offers a practical philosophy for simplifying one's digital life. It pairs well with the Notification Audit and Time Vault strategies discussed in the chapter and offers frameworks for cutting through the noise without abandoning technology altogether.

4. **Irresistible: The Rise of Addictive Technology and the Business of Keeping Us Hooked by Adam Alter**
    Alter peels back the curtain on how digital platforms are intentionally engineered to exploit our attention. This

ties directly to the chapter's insights on dopamine loops and smartphone dependency. Readers who want to better understand the forces working against their focus will find this both eye-opening and empowering.

5. **If Not Now, When? The Effects of Interruption at Different Moments Within Task Execution by Peter Adamczyk & Brian Bailey**
This academic paper adds nuance to the discussion on interruptions by studying how the timing of an interruption affects task performance. It supports the idea that not all interruptions are created equal and strengthens the rationale behind creating structured, uninterrupted work blocks like the Time Vault.

6. **The Cost of Interrupted Work: More Speed and Stress by Gloria Mark, Daniela Gudith, & Ulrich Klocke**
This study provides hard data on how interruptions lead to more hurried and error-prone work—echoing the real-world stories and financial implications discussed in the chapter. It reinforces the notion that constant task-switching undermines both performance and wellbeing.

7. **Deep Work: Rules for Focused Success in a Distracted World by Cal Newport**
This foundational book dives into the power of focused work in a world full of distraction. Newport provides compelling arguments and actionable strategies for carving out uninterrupted time for cognitively demanding tasks. It perfectly complements the Time Vault Strategy and underscores the benefits of sustained attention highlighted throughout this chapter.

8. **Cognitive Control in Media Multitaskers by Eyal Ophir, Clifford Nass, & Anthony Wagner**
   This research explores how chronic multitasking impairs one's ability to filter distractions. It undergirds the chapter's assertion that digital habits reshape neural pathways, making it harder to engage in deep thinking over time. Great for readers wanting the neuroscience behind their multitasking struggles.

9. **Brain Drain: The Mere Presence of One's Own Smartphone Reduces Available Cognitive Capacity by Adrian Ward et al.**
   This provocative study is directly referenced in the chapter and shows how just having your phone nearby— even unused—can diminish your mental sharpness. It's a must-read for anyone skeptical about the impact of digital proximity on performance.

10. **IBrain: Surviving the Technological Alteration of the Modern Mind by Gary Small & Gigi Vorgan**
    This book bridges neuroscience and pop culture to explain how digital media is literally rewiring our brains. It adds depth to the chapter's warning about neural reprogramming and helps readers understand the broader implications of sustained screen exposure over time.

9 | THE CONTROL ILLUSION

"YOU DON'T HIRE SMART PEOPLE TO TELL THEM WHAT TO DO. YOU HIRE SMART PEOPLE SO THEY CAN TELL YOU WHAT TO DO."

– STEVE JOBS –

American entrepreneur, Inventor

HOW MICROMANAGING SIPHONS AWAY VALUABLE TIME

Greg used to believe that the only way to guarantee success was to keep a tight grip on everything in his business. His name was on the line with every decision, every email, every minor task. So, he hovered. Then he corrected. Then he rechecked the work that had already been checked.

What Greg didn't realize was that he was siphoning away his most precious resource: his own time. Instead of working on strategy or growth, he was drowning in details someone else could have handled.

If you've led long enough, you've probably done it too.

Maybe you've caught yourself reviewing every report before it goes out. Or insisting on approving emails to a client. Or jumping into tasks your team should own. That may feel like control—but in reality, it becomes a bottleneck. And worse, it trains your team to wait for you. Over time, they stop thinking for themselves. They hold back. They delay decisions. Progress screeches to a halt because everything has to be funneled through you.

Here's another story that drives the point home.

One of my clients, Chris, told me about an assistant he hired early in his career. Her name was Lisa. Sharp. Efficient. Proactive. One of the best hires he'd ever made. But instead of letting Lisa run with her job, he kept checking her work like his life depended on it. One day, after correcting the grammar in one of her emails (for the second time), Lisa looked up and said, "You know, if you're going to keep doing my job, you might as well put your name on my paycheck."

Ouch. Point taken.

Micromanagement isn't just inefficient—it's expensive. Every minute spent hovering over low-level tasks is a minute routed away from higher-value activities.

> *There's only so much bandwidth in your day and micromanagement eats it like a python in the Everglades.*

The impact doesn't stop with your calendar–there's a team performance side.

When people know their work will be second-guessed—or outright redone—they stop bringing their best. They hesitate. They wait for your correction instead of taking initiative. The team slowly shifts from proactive contributors to passive processors—from rowers to passengers. The more you insert yourself, the more they check out.

This all comes at a financial cost.

Your time as a leader should be spent on things only you can do. Not rewriting emails. Not double-checking spreadsheets. Not creating decision bottlenecks. When you (the leader) stay stuck in the weeds, you rob your organization of its leadership and forward momentum.

The emotional toll isn't small either. Managers who live in the land of over-control often work longer hours, carry more frustration, and begin to resent the very business they built. Micromanagement doesn't just strain your team—it slowly drains your passion.

The research backs this up.

Studies show that nearly 70% of employees under micromanagement experience a drop in morale, and over half report a noticeable decline in productivity. It's not just numbers—there's a ripple effect: stress rises, job satisfaction craters, and engagement withers.

You hired these people because they believed in your vision for your company. But they have a vision for themselves, too, and it's not just about benefits, so the most capable, driven team members don't stick around. They don't stay because of the pay or the perks. They leave because they weren't trusted to do the job they were hired to do.

"Hiring talent remains the number one concern of CEOs [according to] a 2019 survey by the leadership think tank, the Conference Board; CEOs cited finding qualified workers as the largest obstacle to hiring." (Based on responses from 800 CEOs and 600 senior executives)

So, if you've hired the best people, why would you feel the need to micromanage them, expending time, effort and money into an already best bet?

Let this sink in: Micromanagement isn't about perfectionism— it's about control, insecurity and confusion about your own clarity and decision-making ability. You're second-guessing yourself so you constantly try to validate your decisions through checking and rechecking every movement. And the more control a leader chases, the less productive everyone becomes.

If you find yourself saying, "It's just faster if I do it myself," or "No one ever gets it right," then you may already be caught in the micromanagement vortex—where time disappears, trust erodes, and nothing moves forward unless you push it.

It's costing you time, energy, momentum—and maybe even your best people.

To lead well, you have to outgrow the patterns that once served you. And that starts with recognizing where they came from.

THE ROOT OF THE MICROMANAGEMENT STYLE

Micromanagement doesn't usually begin with bad intentions. It often starts as a survival instinct—especially for startups or leaders who came up through the ranks doing everything themselves. For many, it's the only model of leadership they ever saw. The boss who hovered. The manager who double-checked everything. The executive who equated oversight with excellence.

In that kind of environment, control gets mistaken for competence. Precision becomes the priority. And trust? It's a luxury no one feels they can afford.

But there's more to it than just modeling. Micromanagement also takes root when leaders don't know how to transition from doer to delegator. They were promoted for execution, not empowerment. So when things get tense, they fall back on what they know: fix it themselves.

Add in a healthy dose of perfectionism, insecurity, and maybe a past experience where someone dropped the ball—and suddenly micromanagement feels like the only safe option.

Here's the irony: the very instinct that makes leaders clamp down is the one that quietly chokes progress. Control becomes a comfort zone—and like any comfort zone, it eventually becomes a cage.

WHEN CONTROL TURNS TOXIC - A CAUTIONARY TALE

Not all micromanagement is born from insecurity or a noble (if misguided) desire for excellence. Sometimes, it becomes something far more damaging: a weapon of control used to suppress others.

It's one thing to overcorrect a spreadsheet or insist on approving every client email. It's another thing entirely to systematically erode someone's confidence because their competence feels threatening.

I once served under a leader like that. For nearly a decade, I watched as he used control not to guide—but to intimidate. His leadership style wasn't rooted in trust, but in fear. He rarely corrected in private. Fault-finding was his default mode. And if you showed too much initiative, creativity, or autonomy you became a target.

It nearly broke me. Not because I was weak, but because I was capable—and he couldn't stand that.

That kind of leader often doesn't recognize what they're doing. They manage their image upward while quietly crushing the potential of those beneath them. Morale slips. Turnover climbs. Innovation disappears. Eventually, the best people either burn out or move on.

If you're an owner or CEO, here's what you need to know: This kind of micromanagement hides in plain sight. But the signs are always there—suppressed creativity, stagnant culture, and a steady exit of your top performers.

If you see it, don't excuse it. Don't promote it. Don't ignore it.

Call it what it is—and root it out.

Because the cost isn't just time. It's talent. It's trust. And eventually, it's the soul of your team.

ESCAPE THE ILLUSION: A NEW WAY TO LEAD

Breaking free from micromanagement isn't about letting go of excellence—it's about changing how you achieve it. Control might get short-term results, but trust creates sustainable momentum. The shift from hovering to empowering begins with one key question:

"How do I ensure the work gets done well—without having to do it all myself?"

Here's how to make that shift real, practical, and sustainable:

1. Define What "Well-Done" Looks Like

Most micromanagement stems from ambiguity. If no one knows what "good" looks like, you'll always feel the need to step in.

- Document Your Standards:

  If you keep rewriting emails, create a shared template. If reports fall short, provide a standard format. If a process lives only in your head, write it down. Better yet, invite your team to help shape it—they'll likely catch things you've missed.

- Define Success Together:

  Collaboration fuels clarity. When your team helps define what "well-done" means, they're far more likely to deliver it.

> *You can't hold someone accountable for a standard they didn't know existed.*

2. Delegate With Authority, Not Just Tasks

Handing something off isn't the same as delegation. True delegation includes trust, decision rights, and the freedom to act.

- Assign Ownership + Decision-Making Power:

  If your team needs your approval for every move, you haven't delegated—you've just distributed labor. Make it clear where they have full authority and where they need check-ins.

- Use Structured Checkpoints:

  Ease into it. Instead of five approval stages, try three. Instead of daily feedback, move to weekly. You're building muscle memory—for both of you.

3. Coach Instead of Correct

Leadership isn't about doing it better—it's about helping them do it better.

- Coach the Gaps, Don't Fill Them In:

  Instead of rewriting a report, point out two areas to improve and let your team close the loop. This builds capability while freeing your time for higher-order thinking.

- Invite Reflection:

  Ask, "What would you do differently next time?" and watch how quickly confidence begins to grow.

4. Build a Delegation Culture

Trust isn't a talent—it's a system you build.

- Hold a Delegation Review:

Ask your team what they believe they can take on without you. You may be surprised at how much readiness is sitting idle, waiting for permission to lead.

- Create Oversight Boundaries:

  Some work requires your fingerprints. Most doesn't. Identify which tasks truly need your review—and which ones you're just hovering over out of habit.

- Use Tech Wisely:

  Tools like Asana, Monday.com, or Motion.ai help you track without hovering. Set milestones, review asynchronously, and resist the urge to micromanage in the comments.

5. Reclaim Your Time

The real win isn't just delegation—it's redirection. Time saved is only valuable if it's reinvested wisely.

- Recalibrate Your Focus:

  Make a list: What can only you do? Protect those tasks. Everything else? Teach it. Delegate it. Let it go.

- Try a No-Intervention Day:

  One day a week, let the process run without your hand on the wheel. Watch what happens when trust is given room to grow.

- Track the Payoff:

  Each month, reflect: How much time have you reclaimed? What shifted in morale or output? Make it visible. Growth likes to be measured.

CALIBRATION QUESTIONS

1. What am I still holding onto that someone else on my team could handle—with the right clarity and support ?
   → *Invites reflection on lingering control habits and underused team capacity.*

2. Where do I find it hardest to let go—and what fear might be driving that?
   → *Helps surface the root cause behind over-involvement.*

3. How has my instinct to perfect or protect unintentionally slowed growth—for me or for my team?
   → *Connects micromanagement behavior with its hidden costs.*

4. What would change in my business if I stopped over-functioning and started trusting?
→ *Explores the real potential of trust-based leadership.*

5. When have I crossed the line from coaching into correcting—and what impact did it have?
→ *Invites honest evaluation of leadership tone and style.*

6. Which tasks truly require my involvement—and which ones am I clinging to out of habit or fear?
→ *Helps identify the high-value vs. low-leverage divide.*

7. What's one small step I can take this week to build trust
   and reduce bottlenecks in my leadership?
   → *Promotes immediate action toward releasing control.*

*When you do the work of ten, you rob
nine others of the chance to grow.*

FINAL THOUGHTS

Micromanagement often masquerades as diligence, but in
reality, it's a slow siphon—of energy, creativity, and time—for
both you and your team. The irony? The very instinct to make
sure everything is done "just right" ends up sabotaging the
very outcomes you care most about.

Leading well requires trust. And trust isn't built by doing
more—it's built by letting go wisely.

When you shift from control to clarity, from correction to
coaching, you begin to reclaim your calendar and rebuild a
culture where others can rise. Excellence doesn't come from
doing everything yourself—it comes from equipping others to
do great work without you.

So here's the real question:

What might change if you stepped back just enough to let your team show you what they're truly capable of?

RECOMMENDED RESOURCES

1. **The Busy Manager's Guide to Delegation** by Richard Luecke and Perry McIntosh
   This concise, practical guide is perfect for leaders who know they need to delegate more but struggle to do so effectively. It complements Chapter 9 by providing straightforward steps to shift from control to trust—just what the overwhelmed micromanager needs.

2. **Deep and Deliberate Delegation: A New Art for Unleashing Talent and Winning Back Time** by Dave Stitt
   This book reinforces the core message of Chapter 9: leaders must delegate not just to lighten their load, but to empower their team. Stitt offers a fresh take on how purposeful delegation fuels both performance and culture, making it an excellent next step for readers ready to break the control cycle.

3. **If You Want It Done Right, You Don't Have to Do It Yourself! The Power of Effective Delegation** by Donna M. Genett
   Genett's storytelling approach makes this a relatable and highly digestible resource. It supports this chapter's argument that effective delegation is a skill that can be learned—and that mastering it benefits both the leader and their team.

4. **Enabling Empowerment: A Leadership Playbook for Ending Micromanagement** by Shawn Seifert
   Seifert dives straight into the cultural and operational consequences of micromanagement. His guidance echoes the chapter's emphasis on trust and autonomy, offering

tactical solutions to help leaders foster ownership at every level.

5. **Delegating Work (HBR 20-Minute Manager Series)** by Harvard Business Review
Short on time but big on clarity, this resource reinforces many of the practical techniques shared in Chapter 9. It's ideal for busy leaders who need a quick-hit refresher on how to get out of the weeds and elevate their strategic leadership.

6. **Effective Delegation of Authority: A (Really) Short Book for New Managers** by Hassan Osman
This bite-sized book is especially helpful for newer leaders trying to shed the habit of doing it all themselves. It pairs well with this chapter's coaching tone and offers actionable advice for creating more bandwidth without losing control.

7. **My Way or the Highway: The Micromanagement Survival Guide** by Harry Chambers
A deeper dive into the psychology and consequences of micromanagement, this book explains why controlling leaders burn out and drive others away. It's an excellent companion for readers who saw themselves in the cautionary tales of this chapter and want to course-correct.

8. **Multipliers: How the Best Leaders Make Everyone Smarter** by Liz Wiseman and Greg McKeown
This influential book aligns with Chapter 9's premise that great leaders don't hoard intelligence—they multiply it. It's a perfect next step for readers who want to shift from micromanager to talent developer.

9. **Radical Candor: Be a Kick-Ass Boss Without Losing Your Humanity** by Kim Scott
This book challenges leaders to be both caring and candid. It supports the idea that trust and growth are built through honest feedback, not over-control. Especially helpful for readers struggling to shift from correction to coaching.

10. **The One Minute Manager Meets the Monkey** by Ken Blanchard and William Oncken Jr.
This classic illustrates how leaders unintentionally take on everyone else's problems—and how to stop. It supports the chapter's message that rescuing your team from their work doesn't serve them (or you) in the long run.

10 | PERSONAL ENERGY MISMANAGEMENT

"YOUR ENERGY IS UNIQUE. EMBRACE IT. USE IT WISELY. MAKE IT COUNT."

- ROBIN SHARMA -

Author, Speaker

IF TIME IS THE STAGE, ENERGY RUNS THE SHOW

You can have a beautifully structured calendar. Every hour accounted for: Meetings booked, tasks slotted, buffers built in. But if your energy is shot, you won't carry it all effectively.

Fatigue doesn't just slow you down—it warps your judgment, shrinks your patience, and chips away at your confidence. You might show up, but you're not really present. And when presence fades, performance follows.

As a busy professional, your time is precious. Your days are packed with decisions, strategic thinking, and leadership demands. But have you noticed how some hours feel sharp and dialed in—while others blur into a mental fog? That's not a time problem. It's an energy problem.

Here's the hard truth: your business doesn't just need your time. It needs your clearest thinking, your deepest focus, and your best problem-solving capacity.

And those aren't powered by willpower—they're fueled by well-managed energy.

When your energy's high, you make things happen. You think creatively. You solve problems that were gridlocked the day before. But when energy dips even the basics feel like a grind. Communication gets clumsy. Details slip through the cracks. Tempers flare. Mistakes multiply.

> *Productivity might wear a watch, but it runs on sleep, fuel, and focus.*

This is where many leaders get tripped up. We assume time management is about squeezing more in—being faster, sharper, more efficient. But real effectiveness comes from aligning the right work to the right energy.

And one of the simplest—but most overlooked—tools for doing that is learning your personal energy rhythm.

When do you feel most alert? When does your focus fade?

When do you tend to crash? Tracking this doesn't take long, but it can change your whole approach to the day. You stop cramming every hour full and start designing your schedule around that natural rhythm.

Here's the part most folks miss: energy mismanagement doesn't just slow you down, it changes your mindset. It pushes you into reaction mode. Exhausted leaders default to the path of least resistance. They avoid complexity. They stop thinking long-term. They become tacticians instead of strategists. Over time, that stunts progress—and quietly drains your sense of peace. And it also shows up in your team's progress and the culture you allow to develop.

When your energy is depleted, the cracks in your leadership start to show. Conversations become harder to navigate, your tone loses its warmth, and the subtle cues that usually tap your insight slip right past you. Without realizing it, you begin to miss the nuance, the context, the deeper read of the moment. And while these lapses may seem minor, they add up.

> *Energy leaks don't just hinder what you do as a leader, they compromise how you show up. Presence isn't just a bonus in leadership—it's the force that shapes every interaction, decision, and outcome.*

The first fix? Awareness. Observe your rhythms. Respect your limits. Build a schedule that works with your energy instead of against it. That's when your best work starts to surface—and you stop burning yourself out just trying to keep up.

STEWARDING THE SOURCE: WHERE HEALTH AND LEADERSHIP MEET

If time is the stage, and energy runs the show, then it's only fair we ask: What powers my energy?
The answer may be simpler—and more profound—than you think.

Too often, we treat sleep, nutrition, and exercise like lifestyle accessories. Good habits, sure, but optional. Something to circle back to once the business settles down or the kids get older or the inbox gets lighter. The problem? Those things rarely happen. And in the meantime, we're demanding elite performance from bodies and brains we've neglected, overloaded, or taken for granted. It's time for a new frame—one rooted in stewardship.

Your body isn't just a machine that carries your brain from meeting to meeting. It's the physical vessel you've been entrusted with. A gift from The Creator. Designed with breathtaking complexity, this body—and especially your brain—houses your decisions, emotions, focus, and insight. It's what allows you to create, lead, and connect. And just like any high-performance system, it requires care, calibration, and margin.

The human brain is your command center. It governs how you think, how you lead, how you relate. Yet we rarely consider its most basic needs.

> *We wouldn't dream of running our businesses on empty, but many of us attempt to run our lives that way.*

And the cost shows up everywhere: in how we process, react under pressure, how we make decisions, how we listen, and how we lead others.

Over the past decade, I've spent countless hours reading, listening, and learning from some of the leading minds in neuroscience and health—people such as Dr. Andrew Huberman, Dr. Daniel Amen, and Dr. Jordan Rubin. Their research consistently points to one truth: our brains cannot function at optimal levels without consistent attention to three essential inputs—sleep, nutrition, and movement. These aren't bonus habits for high performers. They are the foundation for every living human. Ignore them, and your productivity will always have a ceiling.

And here's what makes it even more sobering: entrepreneurs tax their brains harder than most people ever will—long hours, complex decisions, constant stimulation, emotional load, relentless pressure. Yet we fuel our bodies like we're prepping for a casual stroll, not a full-contact chess match.

This chapter isn't meant to overwhelm you with science or shame. It's meant to awaken something. A conviction that how you care for your physical body is directly connected to how you lead, how you love, and how you show up in the world.

Because once you understand that energy isn't just a feeling—it's a finite resource shaped by your choices—everything changes.

You don't need to just manage time—you need to manage the energy that drives it.

FUEL, FIRE, AND FOCUS

Let's get practical. If your energy is the engine that drives your productivity, then sleep, nutrition, and movement are the three most critical fuels you've got. The problem? Most entrepreneurs treat them like optional extras. Something to circle back to when things calm down. Spoiler alert: they rarely do.

Ignore these core inputs, and your energy turns into a leaky bucket. You may be running full speed—but you're not getting far. Let's break it down.

1. Sleep: A Strategy, Not a Luxury

Sleep is the first to go and the last to be respected. Yet it's the keystone habit that affects nearly every function of your brain.

Consistent, high-quality sleep improves memory, emotional regulation, creativity, and decision-making. Miss it—even by a little—and your cognitive performance starts to unravel. You become slower to process, quicker to react, and more prone to error. Stress feels heavier and small problems get magnified. Leadership presence? Gone. We don't think of sleep as strategic—but it's one of the highest ROI activities in your week. One bad night can dull your edge. A pattern of them can derail your leadership. Leave it unchecked, and you're not just tired—you're on a slow march to burnout disguised as productivity.

2. Nutrition: The Undervalued Leadership Fuel

In the chaos of a packed schedule, it's tempting to treat food like a convenience and the need to eat like a distracting annoyance. Grab whatever's nearby. Power through on caffeine and adrenaline. But your brain is fueled by a delicate chemistry—not by whatever nibble you find to be convenient.

Poor nutrition triggers spikes and crashes in blood sugar, leaving you foggy, irritable, and drained. The real cost is both mental and physical. If you want to think clearly, stay calm under pressure, and make decisions that hold up, you need to eat like a leader:

- Prioritize whole foods—that means foods as close to their original form as possible.
- Aim for stable energy: protein, healthy fats, complex carbs—leave out the vending machine and most industrially processed foods.
- And hydrate—seriously—spring water should always be a first choice, RO (reverse osmosis) filtered, as a second. Limit juices and caffeinated drinks, and eliminate as much as possible sweetened and artificial beverages.

Your brain is roughly 73% water, Water is the most abundant molecule in cells, comprising up to 90% of cell composition. Even mild dehydration can shrink your processing speed and increase fatigue. Water isn't just a nice-to-have. It's the lubricant for your neural circuitry. Without it, your supercomputer overheats.

3. Movement: The Mind Moves Better When the Body Does

Exercise isn't about fitness for its own sake—it's about supporting the physical structure and unlocking your mental edge.

When you move your body, you increase blood flow to the brain, reduce cortisol, and release endorphins that sharpen your mood and attention. You don't need an hour in the gym. A brisk 10–15-minute walk between meetings can recalibrate your mindset, reset your posture, and re-center your thoughts.

Unfortunately, too many leaders treat exercise like an indulgence. It's not. It's a strategic play. One of the best.

HIDDEN ENERGY THIEVES

While we're here, let's name a few of the less obvious culprits stealing your bandwidth:

- Late-night doom scrolling
- Skipped meals
- Overbooked calendars
- Endless screen time without breaks

Each one chips away at your reserves until you're operating in a fog and calling it normal.

WHAT WORKS ISN'T COMPLICATED

If you're serious about raising your energy ceiling—and your effective use of "awake time"—the fundamentals haven't changed:

- Sleep consistently.
- Eat with intention.
- Move your body.

That's it. Not glamorous. Just effective.

Let this sink in.

> *Downtime isn't laziness—*
> *it's leadership maintenance.*

That may be a new lens for you. But the leaders who last, and lead well, are the ones who learn to recharge strategically—not just collapse reactively.

Honor the vessel. Steward the source. And you'll find that clarity, energy, and endurance start showing up when you need them most.

ALIGNING TASKS TO YOUR ENERGY PEAKS

Let's say you wake up, full of clarity and focus—but your calendar greets you with three status meetings, two low-stakes check-ins, and a lunch you didn't ask for. Your most important work? Buried at 2:00 p.m., right as your energy flatlines.
Ring any bells?

Most leaders schedule their days based on availability instead of ability. They organize around logistics instead of leverage. But your peak energy hours are not neutral—they're prime real estate. That's when your brain is firing, your insight is sharp, and your decisions carry weight. Those hours should be treated like gold.

Your high-energy windows are meant for:

- Deep strategic thinking
- High-stakes decisions
- Creative problem-solving
- Crucial coaching conversations

What they're not meant for:

- Inbox purging
- Meeting overflow
- Spreadsheet reviews
- Calendar gymnastics

Save the administrative work and lower-demand tasks for the hours when your energy naturally dips. This isn't laziness—it's leverage.

To do this well, you have to become a student of your own rhythm. Start noticing:

- Does a carb-heavy lunch knock you off course?
- Do back-to-back meetings leave you mentally tapped?
- Does poor sleep sabotage your focus until noon?

These aren't inconveniences—they're signals. And smart leaders pay attention.

Even short breaks during low-energy moments can prevent long-term depletion. A 10-minute walk, exposure to sunlight, a moment of silence, a glass of water—these micro-recoveries create macro returns. Recovery isn't the opposite of productivity. It's part of the cycle.

Here's a simple diagnostic:

For one week, track the following:

- Your energy level at four key points: morning, mid-day, afternoon, evening
- What activity you were doing at each time
- How mentally sharp or focused you felt

At the end of the week, look for patterns. When do you naturally rise? When do you start to dip? That small habit gives you the data to stop guessing—and start planning your day around when you're at your best.

> *You don't need more hours. You need better energy alignment.*

THE PERSONAL ENERGY PROTOCOL

Build your own energy rhythm by locking in these high-leverage habits:

- **Track your energy for one week.** Capture highs and lows throughout the day and note what you were doing. Patterns will surface.
- **Protect your sleep window.** Go to bed and wake up consistently. Power down screens, which stimulate brain activity, one hour before bedtime (that includes smartphones, TVs, computers, tablets, e-readers) and build a simple wind-down routine.
- **Fuel with intention.** Prioritize real food—protein, healthy fats, complex carbs, fiber. Avoid the crashes that come

with sugar and convenience.

- **Hydrate early, hydrate often.** Don't wait for thirst. Your brain is mostly water—treat it that way.
- **Move daily.** Walk. Stretch. Breathe. Do something that reminds your body it's part of the equation.
- **Align your work with your energy peaks.** Save deep work for your sharpest hours. Let email wait.
- **Take real breaks.** Step away, reset, recharge. Even five minutes can restore clarity.
- **Reduce decision clutter.** Automate the basics—meals, wardrobe, routines—so your mental bandwidth stays focused where it matters.

Every great tool deserves to be used, not just read about. Request your **Personal Energy Protocol Worksheet**—and the rest of the **Time Gambit Toolbox**—by emailing **support@ timegambitbook.com** with **"Toolbox Access"** in the subject line, and start aligning tasks to your energy peaks.

> *You won't out-hustle your biology.*
> *Build your habits or bind your limits.*

CALIBRATION QUESTIONS

1. When during the day do I feel the sharpest—and when do I typically fade?
→ *Helps me uncover personal energy peaks and valleys for strategic scheduling.*

2. What parts of my routine are quietly draining my energy?
→ *Reveals hidden habits that lower my performance, such as late-night scrolling or inconsistent meals.*

3. Which of the three core inputs—sleep, nutrition, or movement—needs the most immediate attention?
→ *Creates clarity about where my energy stewardship is weakest.*

4. How often am I doing my most important work during my lowest energy hours?
   → *Prompts honest reflection on whether I'm aligning time and task well.*

5. What physical signals—like mental fog, impatience, or sluggishness—do I tend to ignore when my energy runs low?
   → *Invites awareness around my personal warning signs of depletion.*

6. What's one habit I could implement this week to boost my daily energy?
   → *Encourages me to take immediate, strategic action in one area.*

7. How might better energy management impact the way I lead, decide, and relate to others?

→ *Connects my personal rhythms to my leadership outcomes and relationships.*

*"Exhaustion isn't a badge of honor—
it's a signal that self-leadership
has stalled."*

FINAL THOUGHTS

Time is the container, but energy is the current that carries everything forward. You can stack your calendar with the best of intentions, but if you show up depleted, all you've done is schedule mediocrity. Energy mismanagement doesn't just sap productivity—it reshapes how you think, how you decide, and how you lead.

The real opportunity isn't in cramming more into your hours, but in stewarding the vessel you've been entrusted with—your body, mind, and spirit—so those hours actually count. Sleep, nutrition, movement, and alignment to your natural rhythms aren't luxuries; they're the scaffolding of sustainable leadership. When you guard your energy with intention, you reclaim presence. And presence is where leadership lives.

When it all shakes out, the leaders who endure and make the greatest impact aren't the ones who squeeze the most hours out of the week. They're the ones who learn to honor their energy, channel it wisely, and show up at full strength when it matters most.

> *"You don't rise to the level of your time management. You fall to the level of your energy stewardship."*

RECOMMENDED RESOURCES

1. **When: The Scientific Secrets of Perfect Timing** by Daniel H. Pink
   Pink explores how our biological rhythms influence decision-making, creativity, and focus. It's an excellent companion to this chapter's emphasis on aligning your most important work with your natural energy peaks.

2. **Feel Better Fast and Make It Last** by Dr. Daniel Amen
   Dr. Amen offers actionable steps to improve brain function, emotional resilience, and focus—fast. His work bridges neuroscience, psychology, and faith-based insight, supporting the chapter's emphasis on energy management from the inside out.

3. **The Power of Full Engagement** by Jim Loehr and Tony Schwartz
   This foundational book shifts the focus from managing time to managing energy. It blends science and performance psychology to help leaders understand how recovery, rhythm, and personal energy shape sustainable success.

4. **The Maker's Diet** by Jordan S. Rubin
   Combining ancient wisdom with modern nutritional science, Rubin advocates for a whole-foods, biblically rooted approach to eating. It's a fitting addition to this chapter's case for intentional fuel that supports brain health and leadership vitality.

5. **The Circadian Code** by Dr. Satchin Panda
   A deep dive into the role circadian rhythms play in sleep, metabolism, and cognitive function. Panda's work provides science-backed strategies that support better

energy timing—perfect for leaders building healthier, high-performance routines.

6. **Why We Sleep** by Matthew Walker
   Walker unpacks the science of sleep and its vital role in brain function, emotional resilience, and long-term health. This book reinforces the chapter's case that sleep is a leadership tool—not a luxury.

7. **Built to Move** by Kelly and Juliet Starrett
   This practical guide helps busy professionals reclaim basic physical function through simple movement protocols. It aligns with the chapter's argument that regular movement enhances mental clarity and emotional resilience.

8. **Eat Smarter** by Shawn Stevenson
   A science-backed, habit-friendly guide to using food to fuel your brain and body. Stevenson offers tactical strategies for increasing focus, mood, and performance through smarter nutrition choices.

9. **The 4-Hour Body** by Tim Ferriss
   Though unconventional, Ferriss provides useful experimentation frameworks for optimizing sleep, recovery, and physical energy. Leaders who value self-testing and data will find actionable insights in this performance-focused book.

10. **Huberman Lab Podcast** by Dr. Andrew Huberman
    Neuroscientist Dr. Huberman covers the science of performance, focus, sleep, and recovery. Start with episodes on circadian rhythm, neuroplasticity, or dopamine for insights that directly support this chapter's call to steward the brain.

11. Spark: The Revolutionary New Science of Exercise and the Brain by Dr. John J. Ratey
This breakthrough book explores how movement directly affects learning, mood, focus, and stress resilience. Dr. Ratey makes a compelling, science-backed case that exercise isn't just good for the body—it's essential for peak mental performance.

12. Boundaries for Leaders by Dr. Henry Cloud
Cloud shows how leaders can protect their energy and focus by setting healthy boundaries—with time, people, and expectations. It's a perfect follow-up to this chapter's call to stop leaking energy and start stewarding your attention with intention.

PART TWO
MAKING TIME BEHAVE

In Part One, we mapped the most common hidden forces that waste your time. In Part Two, you'll learn how to gain mastery over them—starting with the truths hiding in plain sight.

11 | THE TIME AUDIT
AWARENESS & ATTENTION

"UNTIL YOU VALUE YOURSELF, YOU WILL NOT
VALUE YOUR TIME. UNTIL YOU VALUE YOUR
TIME, YOU WILL NOT DO ANYTHING WITH IT."

- M. SCOTT PECK -

American Psychiatrist, Author

A successful business runs on clear data—operations, finances, market trends. Yet oddly enough, many leaders fail to track *their most precious, non-renewable asset: time.* It's like driving cross-country without ever checking the fuel gauge—sooner or later, you're going to stall out.

After decades of coaching CEOs and senior executives, I've noticed a consistent pattern. The leaders who consistently excel aren't just aware of their time—they're students of it. They don't rely on guesses or gut feel. They track it. Study it. Audit it.

Here's the truth bomb: even high-performing professionals are often surprised by what a time audit reveals.

> *Time, when measured accurately, becomes a mirror. And what you see in that mirror might be the insight that changes everything.*

Let's look at why—and how—you should conduct your own.

WHY A TIME AUDIT?

Your business probably tracks everything—revenue, expenses, customer satisfaction, performance metrics. But do you know exactly how you, the leader, are spending your hours?

If not, you're flying blind.

Without time data, your productivity strategy leans more on hope than on evidence. And as the legendary football coach Vince Lombardi once said, "Hope is not a strategy."

> *You can't change what you don't track.*

I once worked with Michael, a client who ran a highly successful insurance practice. He was skeptical at first. "I'm already efficient," he said. But after just one week of tracking his time using the method I'm about to show you, the data told a different story. Eight hours a week—yes, eight—were being spent on generating routine client reports. He had a capable team, but he'd never considered delegating that task.

Freeing up those eight hours gave him the additional bandwidth he needed to focus on growth strategies for the practice. He was stunned—maybe even a little embarrassed—when he shared the results in my office.

A time audit reveals where your attention actually goes—not where you think it goes. That's a critical distinction. In fact, research sheds light on this:

- A Harvard Business School study found that CEOs spend over 70% of their time in meetings and just 3% on strategic thinking—despite strategic thinking being the work *only they can do.*
- A McKinsey study revealed that up to 40% of executive time is spent on tasks that could be delegated, automated, or eliminated.
- And according to MIT's Sloan Management Review, leaders often misjudge how their time is spent by as much as 30%—a gap between perception and reality that only hard data can close.

Here's the point: Even the sharpest leaders misjudge where their time really goes. Without data, you're guessing—and guesswork doesn't scale. A time audit replaces assumption with insight, turning vague intentions into actionable clarity.

HOW TO CONDUCT A TIME AUDIT

The process is simple, though far from easy to follow-thru on. For one workweek, document how you spend your time in 15-minute increments. Yes, every 15 minutes. Be granular and record everything, including:

- **Meetings**
  Capture who was present, what was discussed, and how long it took. Don't just log formal calendar blocks—include impromptu ones too.
- **Emails**
  Note how often you check email and how much time you spend responding. It's common to underestimate this category dramatically (exposed in Chapter 3.).
- **Strategy sessions**
  These are your highest-level thinking moments. Track whether they're happening intentionally or getting squeezed between reactive tasks.
- **Admin tasks**
  Include things like approvals, reporting, or expense management. These often sneak into peak hours without us realizing it.
- **Interruptions**
  Jot down what pulled you off track and how long it took to reengage. These disruptions are gold mines for reclaiming focus.
- **Breaks, coffee runs, and spontaneous hallway chats**
  These aren't "bad"—but knowing when and how often they occur helps you assess the rhythm of your day and how much mental white space you're building in.

You're not trying to impress anyone. You're not grading yourself. You're collecting data—real, unfiltered insight into how you invest your hours.

> *Every hour has a name,*
> *whether you assign it or not.*

Many of my clients have chosen to build a spreadsheet that covers the nuances of their office environment and workflows. You can begin with basic columns like these:

- **Time Block**
  Break your day into 15-minute increments. Log start and end times so you can spot patterns across the day or week.
- **Activity Description**
  Be specific. Instead of writing "work," note what kind: replying to emails, reviewing financials, preparing a client pitch.
- **Duration**
  Note how long each activity actually took. This is where you'll often see the difference between intention and reality.
- **Priority Level** (1–3, with ONE being highest)
  Use this to rank how essential each activity was to your core objectives. This helps surface how much time is going to low-value tasks.
- **Energy Level** (1–5, with FIVE demanding the most energy)
  Estimate how mentally or emotionally taxing the task was. This will reveal whether you're matching your best energy to your most important work.
- **Notes or Context**
  Include anything helpful—who you were with, why the task ran long, or what else was competing for your attention at the time.

If you're more tech-savvy, consider a digital time-tracking app. Many of these tools monitor usage patterns automatically. (I will include a few well-known desktop and mobile friendly options at the end of this chapter.) The tracking method is not important; your consistency is.

Track every hour for five consecutive workdays. Then review the data. What are your top three time drains? Where do your best hours go? Which activities deserve more attention—and which ones less?

Expect discomfort. That's okay. That tension is the birthplace of transformation.

FROM DATA TO DECISIONS

The real value of your time audit lies in what you do with it.

One of my business owner clients discovered that nearly 60% of his time was being spent on internal-facing activity— meetings, emails, and team check-ins. Meanwhile, only 10% went toward market research and client relationships, the very areas he claimed were his top priorities.

That realization became a turning point. He restructured his calendar, shortened meetings, and delegated much of the internal communication. Six months later, his company posted its fastest quarter of growth in five years.

Your audit will uncover:

TIME TRAPS

Tasks that consistently consume more time than they deserve.

- **Energy leaks**
  Activities that leave you drained without delivering value.
- **Points of frequent distraction**
  The moments and triggers that regularly pull you off course.
- **Patterns of reactive behavior**
  The ways urgency hijacks your intention—often without you noticing.

It will also show you when you're most focused. Do your sharpest hours fall in the morning? Are afternoon energy dips sabotaging critical work? Are you starting each day on your priorities—or just reacting to whatever screams loudest?

PATTERNS, NOT PERFECTION

Let's be clear: the goal isn't to engineer a perfect day. That doesn't exist. Life happens. Interruptions are real. Kids get sick. Deals fall through.

But when you understand the patterns of your time—where it flows freely and where it leaks—you gain the power to recalibrate and course correct.

Time audits also demystify that constant, nagging sense of being busy but not productive. You begin to see how task-switching, unstructured blocks, and even over-scheduling chip away at your focus.

In Chapter 8, we explored how multitasking chips away at deep focus. But it's not just about switching tasks. Let me reiterate: it's also about how long it takes to recover.

Don't forget that study from the University of California, Irvine which found that after an interruption, it takes an average of 23 minutes and 15 seconds to fully regain focus. That's a massive drain when you add it up across the week. Your time audit makes these hidden recovery costs visible.

TRACKING BOTH SIDES OF LIFE

It's important to include personal time in your audit. Leadership doesn't stop at the office door—and neither do stress, burnout, or distraction. Including evenings and weekends in your time log reveals something your calendar alone never will: *whether your life is sustainable.*

One leader discovered her late-night email habit wasn't about dedication—it was about disruption. Her workdays were riddled with constant interruptions. Once she began protecting her focus time, her evenings slowly became her own again.
This is about more than productivity. It's about rhythm. It's about living and leading in a way that's both effective and human.

We like to think we live in silos. That we can compartmentalize—keep work here, life there. But the truth is, we're integrated beings. Strain in one area eventually bleeds into the other. When your health is fraying, your clarity

CALIBRATION QUESTIONS

1. Where does my time actually go—and how do I know?
→ *Helps me confront the difference between what I assume and what's real.*

2. What patterns—both helpful and harmful—keep showing up in my weekly rhythm?
→ *Encourages me to notice repeated behaviors that either support or sabotage my focus.*

3. Which low-value tasks are still claiming my high-value hours?
→ *Invites me to evaluate whether my time is aligned with what matters most.*

4. How well do my calendar and my priorities match up?

→ *Challenges me to check if I'm living by design or default.*

5. What tasks or conversations have suffered because my attention was divided?

→ *Reminds me to consider the relational and professional cost of multitasking.*

6. Am I honoring my personal time with the same intentionality as my professional time?

→ *Helps me assess how well I'm caring for the whole of my life, not just the work side.*

7. When was the last time I truly looked at the story my time is telling me?
→ *Prompts me to take honest ownership of how I'm showing up—and what needs to change.*

> *You can't make time behave if you never take it to therapy.*

FINAL THOUGHTS:

A one-time audit creates awareness. But rhythm, not rescue, is what changes a leader's life.

Consider making the time audit a quarterly practice. It's your personal P&L statement for time—not just tracking how the hours were spent, but evaluating whether those hours are aligned with what matters most. Each audit gives you a snapshot. But over time, those snapshots become a story: one that either confirms your growth or calls you to course-correct.

You can't change what you won't confront. And you can't lead what you don't first learn to steward.

Time doesn't lie. But it will tell you the truth—if you're willing to look.

TIME TRACKING APPS TO HELP MAKE TIME BEHAVE

Here are several of the top automatic time-tracking apps that are mobile-friendly and offer full functionality across both iOS and Android platforms.

1. **Toggl Track**
   - Mobile App: Available on iOS and Android
   - Syncs across devices: Track time on your phone, then continue on desktop or web
   - Smart features: Includes reminders, idle detection, and offline tracking
   - Reports & analytics: View time summaries and detailed usage reports

2. **RescueTime**
   - Mobile App: Available on both platforms
   - Automatic tracking: Monitors which apps you use and how long you use them
   - Focus tools: Includes alerts and goals to help manage distractions
   - Weekly summaries: Get feedback on how your time is being spent

3. **Clockify**
   - Mobile App: Fully functional iOS and Android apps
   - Manual and automatic time tracking
   - Schedule view: See logged time and plan your day
   - Project/task organization: Great for business use and freelancers

4. TimeCamp
- Mobile App: iOS and Android compatible
- Real-time tracking: Automatically records activity by app or website
- Integrates with tools like Trello, Asana, and Slack
- Geolocation tracking (for field teams or location-based entries)

Each of these apps gives you on-the-go access to time tracking with automatic logging features and insights. If you value mobility or do a lot of work outside the office, these tools make it easy to maintain awareness and accountability from your pocket.

Every minute you own is a vote for the future you're building.

RECOMMENDED RESOURCES

1. **Getting Things Done: The Art of Stress-Free Productivity** by David Allen This classic offers a framework for capturing, clarifying, and organizing tasks that complements the time audit process. Once you've identified where your time is going, Allen's system helps you manage it intentionally—reducing mental clutter and promoting calm, decisive action. It's especially valuable for leaders who feel buried in unstructured work.

2. **Deep Work: Rules for Focused Success in a Distracted World** by Cal Newport
After a time audit reveals how much time is lost to distractions and shallow tasks, Newport's insights will show you how to reclaim focus. His book is a powerful guide to creating stretches of uninterrupted time for your most important work. It pairs naturally with the audit's goal of uncovering wasted effort.

3. **168 Hours: You Have More Time Than You Think** by Laura Vanderkam
Vanderkam's premise mirrors the purpose of the time audit—tracking time to uncover misalignment and unlock possibility. Her research and storytelling make a compelling case that your week holds more capacity than you realize. This book will help you reimagine the structure of your days after seeing your time patterns clearly.

4. **The ONE Thing** by Gary Keller & Jay Papasan
This book supports the audit's core challenge: aligning your time with what matters most. It helps readers zero in on high-impact work and eliminate distractions that dilute

effectiveness. It's a practical next step once time-wasting patterns have been identified.

5. **The Effective Executive** by Peter Drucker
Drucker's timeless wisdom reinforces the value of time audits from a leadership standpoint. He argues that effective executives know where their time goes—and act accordingly. This book provides strategic insight for making high-level time decisions based on evidence, not assumptions.

6. **Thinking, Fast and Slow** by Daniel Kahneman
This book explains how our brain processes information and makes decisions. It's a helpful read after completing a time audit because it reveals the mental shortcuts and biases that often lead us to misuse time or misjudge where it's going. Kahneman's work provides language for understanding the "why" behind time-draining behaviors.

7. **Make Time** by Jake Knapp & John Zeratsky
This playful, practical guide is ideal for anyone who feels like time is slipping through their fingers. It offers easy-to-implement tactics for designing days around focus, energy, and intention. After a time audit, this book offers tools to begin reshaping your daily rhythm.

8. **Beyond the To-Do List** (Podcast, hosted by Erik Fisher)
This long-running podcast explores personal productivity through conversations with authors, coaches, and business leaders. Topics frequently include time audits, workflow optimization, energy management, and attention recovery. It's a perfect way to stay inspired and sharpened as you build a rhythm of regular auditing.

9. **Laura Vanderkam's Blog** www.lauravanderkam.com
   Vanderkam's blog is a treasure trove of real-world time tracking stories, reader-submitted schedules, and practical tips. She blends data and narrative in a way that makes time management feel both approachable and aspirational. It's especially useful if you want to make time auditing a recurring practice.

10. **Essentialism: The Disciplined Pursuit of Less** by Greg McKeown
    McKeown's philosophy aligns tightly with the audit's purpose: doing less, but better. Once you've surfaced the time-wasting obligations or distractions, this book helps you create margin for what matters most. It's about regaining control of your energy through conscious trade-offs.

11. **The Time Management Ninja Blog** by Craig Jarrow
    This blog offers quick, actionable posts on time tracking, prioritization, and productivity without overwhelm. It's a great companion for leaders looking to maintain momentum after completing their first audit. Jarrow's writing style is punchy, practical, and easy to apply.

12. **Tranquility by Tuesday** by Laura Vanderkam
    This follow-up to 168 Hours focuses on building sustainable, weekly habits that align with long-term priorities. It offers nine research-backed rules for creating space for what matters—even when life is busy. It's ideal for leaders who want to shift from reactive time management to proactive rhythm design.

12 | DESIGNING YOUR IDEAL WEEK

THE BLUEPRINT FOR A LIFE THAT WORKS

"A PLAN IS WHAT, A SCHEDULE IS WHEN.
IT TAKES BOTH A PLAN AND A SCHEDULE
TO GET THINGS DONE."

– PETER A. TURLA –

Former NASA rocket designer, Author

THE SURGEON WHO HAD NO TIME

Dr. Michael Bennett left his house every morning before sunrise. His demanding schedule required it. Surgeries, consultations, administrative meetings, and teaching rounds left little room for anything else. Even the short gaps between procedures were swallowed by urgent emails, insurance calls, and last-minute patient and staff needs.

For years, he told himself this was the price of success. His colleagues operated the same way. His patients depended on him. His family understood—or so he thought.

One evening, arriving home far later than promised, he found his wife and son finishing dinner without him. His plate sat cold and untouched. His son barely acknowledged his entrance. His wife gently asked how his day went. His reply was the usual: "Busy." Before he could elaborate, his phone vibrated. It was a second attempt from a colleague needing input on a case. He stepped away to take the call.

When he re-entered the dining room several minutes later, he found it empty. Only Koda, the family dog, remained—glaring up at him in hope of a handout.

The following week, he missed his son's baseball game, despite having promised to leave work early. He might've made it, were it not for an emergency patient that derailed his plans. Later that night, sitting alone in his study, he faced a painful truth: work was consuming his life—all of it.

As he mulled over how to reset things on a healthier track, he realized he didn't just need better time management. He needed a different architecture for his entire week. So, he reached out to a mentor—a retired surgeon and trusted friend—who offered him a piece of advice that stuck:

"You don't find time. You design it."

At first, the idea seemed laughable. Time-blocking in a profession as unpredictable as medicine? But desperation has a way of breaking down resistance.

So, he leaned in. And he asked for accountability.

Within a few weeks, he began to see the impact. He started pre-scheduling deep-focus work, reducing unnecessary commitments, and reclaiming time for family. His stress decreased. His impact increased. He learned that the secret to work-life harmony isn't necessarily working fewer hours—it's designing a week that works.

This chapter builds on the one before it. Professionals don't need more hours—they need more intentionality. Most are surprised by what a time audit reveals. Dr. Bennett was one of those people. And what he discovered is available to anyone willing to take an honest look at where their time is going.

> *Your future habits are built on the scaffolding of your current systems.*

WHEN GOOD INTENTIONS AREN'T GOOD ENOUGH

Most professionals live in reactive mode. Meetings, deadlines, and obligations stack up like dominoes. The day becomes something to survive rather than something to shape. Time slips through the cracks. Work bleeds into evenings and weekends. Personal priorities quietly drift to the sidelines.

And with every new demand comes a fresh round of mental triage:

Should I handle this now or later? What should I bump from the schedule?

This constant negotiation fuels decision fatigue. The mental bandwidth required to navigate an unstructured day is draining—and unsustainable over the long haul.

But what if there's another way?

A well-designed week changes everything. It shifts the leader from reaction to intention. Time gets allocated before it gets absorbed. The calendar becomes a reflection of priorities rather than a graveyard of best intentions. Deep work aligns with peak energy. Family time, exercise, and rest aren't squeezed in—they're baked in.

Because here's the truth: a calendar that isn't intentional will fill itself. And if you don't protect your time, someone else will claim it.

I learned that in the most peculiar way.

It was nearly thirty years ago, during a quick lunch at a small Chinese restaurant I used to frequent outside of Atlanta. I was a young father at the time, just getting my feet under me in one of my first leadership roles. Like most new leaders, I thought staying late and doing more would always lead to better results.

On this particular afternoon, the waiter brought out the check along with the little cellophane-wrapped fortune cookie— pretty standard procedure in most Chinese restaurants. Pulling the wrapper from the cookie, I cracked it open and pulled out that little slip of paper inside. I'd always found this part of the meal a little entertaining and amusing.

This time, though, when my eyes landed on the words opposite the winning lottery numbers, it evoked a different— correction—a very different response. Printed on it was something I never would've expected to see. That little paper became really heavy as I read the words:

Hell is paved with good intentions.

I remember sitting there, holding that little fortune like it had just called me out. Contemplation went much deeper than usual as the smile left my face. Those words stuck with me for days.

When I returned for another lunch a few weeks later, I had pretty much forgotten about that odd experience. At meal's end, here came the same waiter, carrying out the same routine she had probably done a thousand times since I'd last visited.

Handing her my bank card, I snatched the cookie off the tray and had it open within a few seconds. Disbelief washed over me as the hair on my neck stood on end…

The same exact fortune stared at me like a mocking apparition who knew my fate.

Looking around the restaurant for hidden cameras, I realized I was having "a moment" that was anything but amusing. It was more than a coincidence. It was a gut check. A warning shot across the bow. I was chasing good things—but losing track of the best ones.

In that moment, I knew something had to change. I couldn't just keep intending to spend time where it mattered. I had to design a life that actually reflected those intentions.

That little slip of paper was the seed that led me down the path to what I'm sharing with you in this chapter. After all these years, I still have it as a reminder.

> *Designing your week isn't about making everything fit. It's about making what matters most non-negotiable.*

HOW TO CREATE A TIME-BLOCKED WEEKLY SCHEDULE

Designing your ideal week begins with a blank canvas. Rather than starting with tasks, start with categories. These categories are like containers—they give your time shape and function. They prevent leaks and allow you to align each moment with what matters most.

1. **Identify Core Priorities**
   Before you can block time, you have to know what deserves it. What goals are most meaningful right now? What outcomes truly move the needle in your personal and professional life? Your schedule should reflect your answers to these questions.

   (To build on what we explored in Chapter 7, your calendar should become a living reflection of your vision, purpose, and values. Otherwise, it just becomes a to-do list with no soul.)

2. **Define Time Categories**
   Not all work is created equal. Some tasks require intense concentration. Others involve collaboration or routine follow-through. When these blend together, chaos reigns.

Time categories bring clarity:

- Deep Work: Strategy, problem-solving, creative projects, high-focus deliverables.
- Shallow Work: Emails, admin, logistics, reporting.
- Meetings: Client sessions, team standups, leadership check-ins.
- Personal Time: Exercise, spiritual practices, hobbies, time with family.
- Rest and Recovery: Sleep, breaks, solitude, margin.

Each of these deserves a place on your calendar. Otherwise, urgency will hijack your agenda before your priorities ever get a chance to speak.

3. **Align Work with Energy Levels**
   Your brain doesn't run at full capacity all day. Cognitive energy ebbs and flows. The most intellectually demanding work should land during your high-energy hours.

If you've done the work from Chapter 11 (and its accompanying worksheet available for download), you're already on your way to identifying those peak hours. Most people experience their mental peak in the morning—use it for deep work. Afternoons are better suited for meetings or collaboration. Evenings are ideal for planning, creative drift, or winding down.

Honor your rhythms. Don't require your tired brain to do your most important thinking.

This principle is reinforced by research from Daniel Pink, author of When: The Scientific Secrets of Perfect Timing, who found that aligning tasks with natural energy cycles improves both performance and mood.

(This step naturally builds on the work you began in Chapter 11. Once you've audited your time and identified your energy rhythms, this is where it all comes together.)

4. **Set Fixed Time Blocks**
Once you've identified your categories and rhythms, assign them real estate on your calendar. Be specific:

- Deep work blocks early in the day.
- Meetings batched into limited windows.
- Admin time set for late afternoon.
- Family time locked in before the day fills up.

A strong system doesn't make decisions for you—it makes your best decisions easier to repeat.

Time gets anchored before the tide of the week rolls in.

5. **Build in Flexibility**
A rigid schedule is a brittle schedule. Emergencies happen. Priorities shift. That's life.

Make space for the unexpected. Add buffers between meetings. Reserve overflow slots for work that spills past its window.

This is where the right technology can shine. Tools like Motion.AI (www.usemotion.com) ensure your important tasks don't fall away—they simply move to the next appropriate and available time slot. Flexibility makes your system sustainable. Without it, one disruption can wreck your entire day.

6. **Establish Non-Negotiables**
   Time blocks only work if you defend them. People will always want more of your time. If your default is to say "yes," your calendar will be overrun.

   Decide in advance what is non-negotiable. For example:

   • No meetings before 10 a.m.
   • Weekly date night with your spouse.
   • Morning workouts on Monday, Wednesday, Friday.

   Once your values are anchored in your calendar, you no longer have to debate them. Others will learn to respect your boundaries—because you've chosen to honor them first.

7. **Automate and Delegate**
   A well-planned week isn't just about what you do—it's also about what you don't do.

   • Delegate low-leverage tasks.
   • Automate recurring activities.
   • Use tools and systems to handle the repetitive so you can focus on the strategic.

(After reading Chapter 9, this shouldn't surprise you: the more you delegate low-leverage tasks, the more you empower your team—and reclaim your leadership focus.)

It's the difference between a leader who is busy and a leader who is effective.

If someone else can do it 80% as well, hand it off.

8. End Each Week with a Review

Don't just plan your week—learn from it. A weekly review is the compass that keeps you aligned.

Ask yourself:

- What went better than expected?
- What distracted me?
- Where did I slip into reaction mode?
- What one tweak could improve next week?

Even a five-minute reflection each Friday can multiply your effectiveness. It's like sharpening the saw before cutting more wood *(a sharp saw cuts more wood faster, expending far less energy.)*

The goal isn't to schedule every minute—it's to give every hour *a purpose.*

With time blocks in place, you stop wondering when you'll get around to that big project or whether you can squeeze in a workout. Your calendar tells you.

CALIBRATION QUESTIONS

1. How often do I feel like my week is happening to me instead of being designed by me?
→ *Helps identify whether you're operating reactively or proactively with your time.*

2. Which parts of my week consistently get neglected, even though I claim they matter?
→ *Surfaces the disconnect between stated values and scheduled priorities.*

3. When am I usually at my sharpest mentally—and how well am I protecting that time?
→ *Encourages alignment of deep work with peak cognitive energy windows.*

4. What's one recurring activity I need to automate, delegate, or eliminate altogether?

→ *Pushes toward reducing low-leverage commitments and reclaiming margin.*

5. What boundaries have I failed to establish that would immediately improve my weekly flow?

→ *Exposes where people-pleasing, overcommitment, or lack of clarity may be undermining schedule integrity.*

6. When was the last time I ended a week feeling proud of how I spent my time?

→ *Invites reflection on effectiveness and peace, not just productivity.*

7. If someone looked at my calendar, would they be able to tell what I value most?

→ *Asks the tough question of whether your schedule actually reflects your intentions.*

The more you plan with purpose, the less you apologize with regret.

FINAL THOUGHTS

Dr. Bennett's life didn't change because he found more time—he changed because he designed the time he had. He became more effective at work, more present at home, and more grounded personally. He didn't just manage his time—he mastered it by shaping it with purpose.

The truth is, a chaotic calendar isn't a badge of honor. It's often just the byproduct of neglect. Time, once spent, is gone for good. But time invested intentionally yields exponential returns.

When you design your week with intention, you build a life that works—not just for your goals or your business, but for your well-being, your relationships, and your peace.

> *Designing your ideal week isn't just a productivity hack. It's an act of stewardship.*

You've been entrusted with a limited number of hours. What you do with them will always reveal what you value most. Every block on your calendar is a brick in the life you're building. Make sure each one is laid with intention.

Tools for Planning and Execution

Structure is easier to maintain with the right tools. Use digital platforms to bring your ideal week to life:

- **Google Calendar:** Color-code your categories. Visual clarity boosts follow-through.
- **Motion.AI:** Uses AI to optimize your schedule, significantly reducing decision fatigue.
- **Notion:** Track your goals, progress, and reflections in one place.
- **Sunsama:** A daily planner that integrates tasks and calendar.
- **RescueTime:** Tracks where your time actually goes—great for honest audits.

Remember, it's not about the tools—it's about consistency. Choose the one that best supports the way your mind wants to work.

RECOMMENDED RESOURCES

1. **When: The Scientific Secrets of Perfect Timing** by Daniel Pink
   This book is grounded in science and teaches the importance of aligning activities with your body's natural rhythms. Pink's research underpins the chapter's guidance on matching energy levels with task types. It's an indispensable resource for anyone designing a schedule that supports peak performance.

2. **The ONE Thing** by Gary Keller
   Keller teaches how to identify the single most important task that makes everything else easier or unnecessary. This concept is essential when identifying core priorities and creating non-negotiable time blocks. It reinforces the idea of designing your week around what truly drives results.

3. **Free to Focus** by Michael Hyatt
   This book offers a complete framework for escaping distraction and reclaiming time for high-leverage activities. Hyatt emphasizes the importance of eliminating low-value tasks, aligning energy with output, and planning weekly with intention. It's a natural companion to this chapter's system of time-blocking and prioritization.

4. **Make Time** by Jake Knapp and John Zeratsky
   A refreshingly tactical book filled with simple strategies to "make time" for what matters most. The authors present a flexible system rooted in focus, energy, and intentional design of your daily and weekly schedule. It aligns directly with this chapter's message: your best time doesn't appear—it's made.

5. **Mind Your Time** by Megan Hyatt Miller (Podcast Episode – Lead to Win)
   In this episode, Megan Hyatt Miller shares strategies for protecting focused time, setting boundaries, and building energy-aware work routines. It speaks directly to the real-life implementation of a time-blocked week. Leaders will especially resonate with how the podcast blends margin, mission, and method.

6. **Time Management for Mortals Blog** by Oliver Burkeman
   This blog—and Burkeman's broader writing—pushes against the myth of total productivity. His insights will challenge readers to focus not on doing more, but on doing what matters most within the limits of their week. His work echoes the stewardship mindset that closes this chapter.

7. **The Full Focus Planner Blog** (FullFocus.co)
   Updated weekly with actionable articles about time-blocking, goal setting, and planning rituals. These resources extend the ideas from this chapter with highly tactical advice for designing and defending a productive week. Particularly helpful for those building the weekly review habit described near the end of the chapter.

8. **Clockwise Podcast** by Productivityist
   This short-format podcast dives into topics like smart scheduling, automation tools, and time stewardship for busy professionals. Its emphasis on creating intentional routines supports the practical strategies discussed in this chapter. The episodes on calendar batching and mental bandwidth are especially aligned.

9. **168 Hours** by Laura Vanderkam
    Vanderkam's central argument—that we all have the same 168 hours per week—calls readers to audit and realign how they spend that time. Her examples show how professionals and parents alike can reclaim time for what matters. This resource strengthens the case for weekly design and intentionality. ⌐¬ SEP⌐

10. **The 12 Week Year** by Brian Moran and Michael Lennington
    This book introduces a powerful planning model that treats each 12 weeks as its own year. Its emphasis on focused execution, time-blocking, and weekly reviews pairs well with the rhythms this chapter promotes. It challenges readers to compress their goals and schedule with urgency and precision.

11. **The Time-Block Planner** by Cal Newport
    While we've excluded Deep Work for redundancy's sake, Newport's Time-Block Planner deserves its own spotlight here. It offers a practical system that turns abstract priorities into scheduled action. For those ready to implement a visual, analog method for ideal week planning, this is a go-to guide.

12. **Building a Second Brain** by Tiago Forte
    This book focuses on how to externalize your thinking, organize your ideas, and reduce mental clutter through digital systems. Forte's approach pairs well with the automation, delegation, and reflection elements of this chapter. His system helps ensure your planning doesn't just stay theoretical—it becomes repeatable.

13 | BUILDING HIGH-PERFORMANCE HABITS
PURPOSEFUL LIVING

"WE ARE WHAT WE REPEATEDLY DO. EXCELLENCE, THEN, IS NOT AN ACT, BUT A HABIT."

- WILL DURANT -

American Historian and Philosopher

THE FREELANCER TRAPPED IN HER OWN CHAOS

Maya loved her work. As a freelance designer, she thrived on the creativity and flexibility. She could choose projects that inspired her, set her own hours, and steer clear of the soul-crushing confines of corporate life. But flexibility, she would learn, came with a hidden cost. Without a structured routine, her days began slipping through her fingers like sand.

She often woke up late, reached for her phone before even getting out of bed, and scrolled through social media while promising herself she'd start work soon. But soon was slow to arrive. Hours evaporated. By afternoon, deadlines loomed like storm clouds—and then the panic would kick in. She'd cram her work into long, frantic sprints, skipping meals and sacrificing sleep just to meet the bare minimum. Morning came too quickly, ushering in another cycle of chaos.

She blamed herself. Maybe she just wasn't disciplined enough. In a burst of motivation, she downloaded the latest productivity apps, mapped out detailed daily routines, and swore she'd become a morning person. And for a few days, things looked promising. She even told her peers how her new system was finally working. But the results never stuck. Every attempted pivot felt like pushing a boulder uphill. She admired those mythical creatures who exercised before sunrise, glided through their routines, and hit their goals like clockwork. For Maya, consistency felt elusive at best—like chasing wind.

> *Most people don't wrestle with time—*
> *they surrender to it.*

One evening, shredded by another chaotic week, she vented to a friend. "I just need more willpower," she sighed. Her friend chuckled. "Willpower doesn't build habits," he said. "Systems do."

Then he told her about the domino effect—how one small habit shift can trigger a cascade of positive change.

Skeptical but desperate, Maya made a single change. She started placing her phone in another room overnight. The first morning, something strange happened. Without the instant dopamine hit of social media, she got out of bed more quickly. That led to a little stretching. Then a short planning session. Within a few weeks, her entire schedule began to reshape itself.

The shift wasn't dramatic. It was quiet. Subtle. But once the first domino fell, other changes would soon follow.

HIDDEN LOOPS THAT RUN YOUR LIFE

Most people assume that if they could just muster more discipline, they'd finally become productive. But discipline is fickle. Motivation rises and falls. Willpower wilts under pressure. Without habits in place, time slips into a pattern of inefficiency—and often, self-sabotage.

Habits, on the other hand, drive automatic behavior. The brain, always seeking to conserve energy, turns repeated actions into shortcuts. These neural pathways free us from constant decision-making. The more often we perform a behavior, the less effort it demands. It's a brilliant feature of the human brain—but it works both ways.

This is why bad habits feel effortless, and good ones feel like pushing a string from the trailing end. One is automated. The other is aspirational.

Neuroscience offers helpful insight here. In The Power of Habit, Charles Duhigg unpacks what he calls the "habit loop." Every habit, he explains, runs on a predictable cycle: cue → routine → reward. A cue triggers the behavior. The behavior itself is the routine. And the reward is the payoff your brain receives. Do this loop enough times, and the brain starts craving the reward at the very moment the cue shows up—*before the behavior even begins.* That craving is what cements the loop and makes it automatic.

Take a common example: constantly checking email.

- The cue? Boredom or anxiety.
- The routine? Clicking open the inbox.
- The reward? A fleeting sense of productivity or escape.

Do it enough, and your brain starts scanning for excuses to open your email—just to get the fix.

So, when we talk about breaking a bad habit—or building a better one—we're not just talking about changing the routine. We also have to address the cue and the reward. That's where most time management advice misses the mark. It focuses on behavior without addressing the brain's wiring beneath it. Maya didn't overhaul her life with some elaborate system. She simply disrupted the loop. By removing the cue—her phone—she made space for a new routine to take root. And that made all the difference.

A bad habit is a loop that your brain automated without your permission.

PRACTICAL HABIT-BUILDING STRATEGIES

High-performance habits aren't powered by inspiration. They're built on structure. The highest-achieving professionals don't wait to feel ready. They engineer their environments and routines to nudge themselves toward excellence and productivity.

1. Habit Stacking

One of the simplest ways to build a new habit is to piggyback it onto an existing one. Instead of creating something from scratch, you attach it to a behavior you're already doing. James Clear, in his book Atomic Habits, popularized this approach as "habit stacking." His insight: when you tie a new habit to an existing routine, you create a predictable cue that increases the likelihood of follow-through.

It might look something like this:

- After I pour my morning coffee → journal for five minutes.
- After brushing my teeth → review my top three priorities.
- After sitting down at my desk → begin with my highest-priority task.
- After sending an email → close my inbox to protect my focus.

This strategy taps into existing neural pathways, reducing cognitive friction. By anchoring a new habit to something already automatic, you leverage your brain's wiring instead of fighting against it. It becomes part of your flow—not just another task to remember.

2. Identity-Based Habits

Willpower-based goals often fizzle out because they focus on what we want to do, not who we want to be.

- "I want to wake up earlier" is fragile.
- "I'm the kind of person who starts the day strong" is foundational.

When your behavior aligns with your identity, consistency becomes easier. Identity shapes decisions before they even reach the conscious level.

Try taking three minutes to jot down a few identity-based declarations around a recent (failed) attempt to build a habit:

- "I'm the type of person who plans before acting."
- "I protect my time and energy for deep work."
- "I prioritize long-term success over short-term dopamine hits."

Each time you make a choice that aligns with these declarations, you reinforce them. Over time, those small decisions shape who you become.

3. Environmental Design

Your surroundings shape your behavior more than you realize. A cluttered desk or noisy space quietly sabotages your focus. But small shifts in your environment can unlock major improvements in behavior.

- Keep your phone in another room during focused work.
- Post a visible task list on your desk.

- Silence all laptop notifications.
- Set visual cues—like an open notebook or a timer—to signal deep work.

Optimizing your environment to support high-value activities isn't just helpful—it's essential. Your space should invite the behaviors you want to repeat.

4. **Implementation Intentions**
High performers don't leave good habits to chance. They pre-decide their behavior using "implementation intentions." These are simple if–then statements that remove ambiguity and lower resistance.

Behavioral psychologist Peter Gollwitzer's research in the 1990s showed that people are significantly more likely to follow through on a goal if they decide in advance when and where they'll act.

Examples:

- If I finish a meeting early → I'll review my priorities.
- If I feel distracted → I'll take a five-minute walk.
- If I hesitate to begin → I'll start with two minutes of effort.

You've already written the script. Now you just follow it.

5. **The 2-Minute Rule**
Big habits often collapse under their own weight. The 2-Minute Rule, also from Atomic Habits, helps sidestep this problem. The premise: make the first step so easy it's nearly impossible to justify not doing it..

- Read one sentence instead of committing to an hour.
- Write a paragraph instead of a whole chapter.
- Review one slide instead of finishing the entire deck.

Once you're in motion, inertia starts working in your favor. Momentum becomes your ally.

6. Accountability Loops

We're more likely to follow through when someone else knows our intention. The fear of disappointing others is often stronger than the discomfort of disappointing ourselves.

In my years of facilitating peer advisory groups, I've heard it again and again: "I got it done because I knew I'd have to report back." The accountability loop made the difference.

Here are a few simple ways to create one:

- Share your goal with a friend, mentor, or coach—and ask them to check in.
- Use visual progress trackers or charts in plain sight.
- Set up automated reminders or recurring status updates.

Creating a loop of gentle pressure turns intention into execution.

7. Reward Systems

Our brains are wired for reward. If something feels good, we're more likely to repeat it. The trick is to align rewards with your desired behaviors—without letting the reward become the distraction.

- Finish a deep work sprint? Take a 10-minute walk outside.
- Hit a weekly milestone? Treat yourself to something small.
- Maintain a habit for a month? Celebrate the win.

A well-placed reward can cement a loop—but only if the reward serves the behavior, not the other way around.

8. Eliminating the Default Options

Bad habits thrive because they're easy. When the path of least resistance leads to distraction, the solution isn't more self-control—it's raising the resistance.

- Unsubscribe from non-essential emails and newsletters.
- Use spam filters to declutter your inbox.
- Remove social media apps or silence notifications during work hours.
- Automate or delegate repetitive tasks when possible.

The goal isn't to fight your defaults. It's to replace them.

THE POWER OF HABIT-DRIVEN TIME MANAGEMENT

Time management isn't about superhuman willpower or color-coded calendar blocks. It's about design. Specifically, designing your days so that good habits become nearly inevitable, and bad habits become frustratingly inconvenient.

The truth is, most people don't have a time problem—they have a habit placement problem. The friction is in the wrong places. Scrolling social media is easy. Prepping for tomorrow is hard. One's a reflex. The other takes effort.

Here's the move that changes the game: small shifts, repeated with consistency, create exponential impact. One small habit—executed at the right moment—can tilt the momentum of an entire day. That's the domino effect at work. It starts quiet, almost invisible. But it scales quickly.

The people who seem to master their time aren't necessarily smarter, faster, or more driven. They're simply more intentional. They know what works and they repeat that. They've stopped relying on mood or motivation. Instead, they build systems—structures that reinforce the outcomes they care about.

Over time, those systems become scaffolding for success. A five-minute planning ritual leads to better meetings. A no-phone morning policy leads to deeper work. A weekly review leads to better decision-making. None of these sounds revolutionary. But stack them together, and they compound into something far greater than the sum of their parts.

In the end, you don't need more hours—you need fewer leaks. And the best way to stop the leaks is to align your habits with your highest values.

CALIBRATION QUESTIONS

1. What habit loop in my life currently keeps me stuck in reactive behavior?
→ *Invites awareness of automated patterns that drive unproductive responses.*

2. Which identity-based habit would make the biggest impact on my daily decisions?
→ *Encourages alignment between values and behavior through identity framing.*

3. What's one environmental change I could make today that would improve my focus?
→ *Highlights how immediate surroundings affect clarity and concentration.*

4. Where am I relying too heavily on motivation instead of structure?
   → *Exposes areas of inconsistency and opportunity for system-based support.*

5. In what way is my current environment silently shaping my behavior—and what's one change I could make to better align it with my goals?
   → *Prompts reflection on subtle environmental cues and how to redesign them.*

6. Who can I invite into an accountability loop to help reinforce a new habit?
   → *Encourages relational support and outside reinforcement for follow-through.*

7. What positive reward could I attach to a consistent behavior I'm trying to build?

→ *Reinforces habit formation through intentional and meaningful reinforcement.*

The future you want is hiding in the habits you haven't built yet.

FINAL THOUGHTS

High-performance habits don't demand superhuman effort—they demand thoughtful design. When we intentionally shape our routines, environments, and identities, we create momentum that starts doing the heavy lifting for us.

The beauty of habit-building is in its compounding power. Small changes—repeated with intention—can spark massive transformation over time.

And it all begins with one well-placed domino.

RECOMMENDED RESOURCES

1. **Atomic Habits** by James Clear
   This book provides a deep dive into the science of habit
   formation and introduces simple, actionable strategies
   such as habit stacking and identity-based behaviors. It
   aligns directly with the chapter's message that systems,
   not willpower, shape behavior. Clear's work reinforces
   the idea that small changes, consistently applied, lead to
   massive transformation.

2. **The Power of Habit** by Charles Duhigg
   Duhigg unpacks the neurological loop of cue, routine,
   and reward, which mirrors the framework discussed in
   this chapter. His engaging storytelling illustrates how
   deeply ingrained habits are formed and how they can be
   intentionally disrupted. It supports the chapter's emphasis
   on changing the full loop—not just the routine.

3. **Deep Work** by Cal Newport
   Newport champions the value of sustained, focused
   attention in a distracted world. His ideas support the
   chapter's encouragement to eliminate digital distractions
   and design environments conducive to productivity.
   The concept of "deep work" complements the chapter's
   strategies like environmental design and focus blocks.

4. **Essentialism by** Greg McKeown
   This book challenges readers to pursue less but better,
   echoing the chapter's call to eliminate default options
   and distractions. McKeown provides clarity on what truly
   matters, helping readers protect their time and energy. It
   aligns especially well with the section on identity-based
   habits and long-term priorities.

5. **Tiny Habits** by BJ Fogg
   Fogg introduces a method of behavior change rooted in starting small—directly reinforcing the 2-Minute Rule from the chapter. He emphasizes the importance of anchoring new habits to existing routines, supporting both habit stacking and momentum-building strategies. Fogg's research validates the principle that easy is sustainable.

6. **The Tim Ferriss Show** (Podcast)
   This podcast features high performers across industries who share routines, experiments, and systems they use to optimize life. Ferriss often discusses implementation intentions and reward systems—ideas central to this chapter. It's an excellent source of real-world application and inspiration for habit formation.

7. **Your Brain at Work** by David Rock
   Rock unpacks how our brains handle tasks, distractions, and focus—grounding many of the chapter's insights in neuroscience. His work supports the discussion on why habits automate behavior and how to align brain chemistry with productivity. Especially helpful for understanding internal resistance and cognitive fatigue.

8. **Make Time** by Jake Knapp and John Zeratsky
   This book offers clear, practical strategies to reclaim time and attention, which reinforce many of the chapter's time design concepts. It's particularly aligned with the environmental design and reward system strategies discussed. The tone and examples make it an accessible, actionable resource.

9. **Getting Things Done** by David Allen
   Allen's GTD methodology helps break down overwhelming tasks into manageable actions, much like the implementation intentions covered in this chapter. His emphasis on capturing ideas and clearing mental clutter pairs well with building high-performance habits. It's a classic system for creating reliable structure and follow-through.

10. **The One Thing** by Gary Keller
    Keller homes in on the importance of prioritization, which complements the chapter's emphasis on identity-based decisions and eliminating distractions. He teaches readers to focus on the task that makes everything else easier or unnecessary—a core idea behind momentum and structured progress. This book is a rally cry for focus in a world of overload.

11. **Nir Eyal's Blog** (nirandfar.com)
    Eyal writes about behavior design, digital distraction, and habit engineering, echoing several core ideas from this chapter. His techniques for resisting triggers and designing better routines tie into implementation intentions and environmental cues. It's a valuable resource for staying consistent in a tech-saturated world.

12. **Hurry Slowly (Podcast)** by Jocelyn K. Glei
    This podcast explores productivity through the lens of intentionality and presence—perfect for reinforcing the chapter's slower-is-faster approach. Topics like creative routines, rest, and mindful time use pair well with habit design and energy management. It encourages the kind of deep, reflective work habits discussed here.

14 | LEVERAGING TECHNOLOGY FOR TIME MASTERY

LEARN TO ELIMINATE WASTED MOTION

"NEVER MISTAKE MOTION FOR ACTION."

– ERNEST HEMINGWAY –

American journalist, novelist, and short-story writer

THE TETRIS SYNDROME: FIVE APPS—ZERO PROGRESS

Alicia glanced at her phone before getting out of bed. Thirty unread emails greeted her like morning traffic—predictable, exhausting, and entirely too early. By the time she reached the office, the number had doubled. A project update from a client, a scheduling conflict, a spreadsheet that urgently needed review—it all blended into a chaotic hum in her brain.

Her calendar looked like a Tetris board with no winning move—meetings stacked on meetings. Quick check-ins were anything but. Follow-ups on follow-ups. Her task list lived in five different apps—Trello, Slack, Asana, her inbox, and the whiteboard by her desk. Ironically, she spent more time managing work than actually doing it. By Friday morning, she had clocked over fifty hours—but her most important project had received no meaningful attention.

One evening, while venting to a colleague over tacos and fatigue, Alicia confessed she was drowning in busywork. "I just need more hours in the day," she sighed.

Her colleague chuckled. "You don't need more hours… you get the same as the rest of us. What you need is a better system."

That conversation set in motion a long-overdue mind-shift. Skeptical but desperate, Alicia started asking questions— leaning on peers who seemed more organized and a whole lot less stressed. She even hired a business coach.

What followed weren't massive overhauls, but simple, intentional changes. She automated email sorting. Adopted an AI scheduling assistant to dodge the endless back-and-forth. Identified repetitive tasks and handed them off to digital tools. Within weeks, she had reclaimed ten hours from her calendar—enough to stop working evenings altogether.

Technology didn't just make her faster. It made her freer. What once felt like digital chaos now functioned like a personal assistant—quietly managing the noise and leaving her energy intact for what mattered most.

TOOLS TO STREAMLINE TIME MANAGEMENT

Used well, technology amplifies focus and flow. Used poorly, it pulls us into digital quicksand.

Technology can be a lever or a leash.

Most professionals collect tools like souvenirs—but without a plan. A new app promises productivity, but without integration, it just becomes another tab in an already cluttered browser.

The right tools act like an invisible assistant—managing routine tasks, educing cognitive drag, and minimizing unnecessary decision-making. When effectively integrated, these tools eliminate wasted motion.

Here's where to start:

- **AI Assistants**
  These digital helpers can take over routine scheduling, sift through your emails, and even compile reports. By reducing the number of minor decisions you make each day, they create a mental buffer—preserving your energy for higher-level tasks. Instead of getting bogged down in logistics, you can redirect your attention toward strategy and leadership.

- **Task Automation**
  Automation tools eliminate the need to perform manual, repetitive steps across your workflow. From auto-populating spreadsheets to sending follow-up emails, task automation doesn't just save time—it reduces the chance of human error. The real win is consistency. Tasks get done the same way every time, freeing you from micromanagement.

- **Calendar Optimization**
  Tools that manage your calendar don't just book meetings—they help defend your focus. With smart rules and preferences, they preserve deep work blocks, reduce back-and-forth scheduling, and protect you from the chaos of double bookings. In the end, they help your day keep its

rhythm—so your productivity can stay in flow.

- **Email Filtering**
  Intelligent filtering systems act like digital gatekeepers—letting only the most important communications reach your eyes. You spend less time scanning subject lines and more time acting on what actually matters. The result? Lower stress, clearer priorities, and yes—Inbox Zero becomes a real possibility.

- **Focus and Distraction Blockers**
  These tools silence digital noise—blocking social media alerts, rogue tabs, and other productivity killers. By eliminating interruptions before they happen, they create an environment where deep, meaningful work can thrive. For many professionals, the difference in output feels almost magical.

- **Project Management Systems**
  Centralizing communication, task tracking, and documentation in one platform creates transparency and alignment. Everyone knows what needs to be done, by when, and by whom. Instead of chasing updates, the team spends their energy executing.

The real win isn't having the best tool; it's making sure the tool serves the system. Used improperly, even a great tool can create a wilderness experience.

AI ASSISTANTS AND TASK AUTOMATION

AI-powered tools are no longer a novelty—they're a necessity. Instead of juggling low-value tasks, digital assistants handle the admin so your brain can stay in strategic mode.

Here are a few standouts worth exploring:

- **Motion.ai** – More than a smart calendar, Motion combines task management, project planning, and scheduling into a single interface. It automatically prioritizes and schedules tasks based on deadlines, focus time, and availability—turning your calendar into a real-time execution plan.

- **Reclaim.ai** – Designed to preserve your deep work blocks, Reclaim integrates with your calendar to automatically defend time for heads-down tasks, routines, and breaks. It can also auto-schedule habits like workouts or admin catch-up—adjusting them dynamically as your schedule changes.

- **SaneBox AI** – This smart inbox filter learns your email habits and automatically diverts unimportant messages to a separate folder, allowing your primary inbox to stay clean and focused. It also sends reminders to follow up on unanswered messages and can even pause your inbox entirely during deep work windows.

- **x.ai** – This AI-powered scheduling assistant handles the entire back-and-forth of setting up meetings. You simply CC the assistant in an email and it proposes, negotiates, and confirms meeting times on your behalf—saving time and reducing friction in client or team coordination.

- **Superhuman** – Built for speed and clarity, Superhuman offers blazing-fast email with AI-powered triage. It prioritizes messages by importance, suggests replies, and includes keyboard shortcuts, split inboxes, and undo-send features—making inbox zero actually achievable.

These tools won't think for you, but they'll protect the mental runway you need to make better decisions.

Now enter the world of automation platforms—the silent workhorses that streamline everything behind the scenes:

- **Zapier** – Zapier connects over 6,000 apps to create automated workflows without writing a line of code. You can trigger actions like copying attachments to cloud storage, syncing CRM updates, or sending Slack alerts— all based on events happening in your other tools.

- **IFTTT (If This, Then That)** – Ideal for personal productivity and simple cross-platform workflows, IFTTT creates conditional automations like "If I star an email, then add it to my to-do list" or "If I post to Instagram, then back it up to Google Drive." It's a lightweight way to reduce repetitive work.

- **TextExpander** – This tool turns a few typed characters into full sentences, paragraphs, or templates. Whether you're replying to emails, documenting procedures, or onboarding new clients, it ensures consistency and speed—especially for repeated phrases or detailed instructions.

- **Grammarly** – Beyond grammar and spelling, Grammarly offers real-time suggestions on tone, clarity, conciseness, and even delivery. It's like having an editor ride shotgun— perfect for professionals who want to sharpen their communication while saving time.

Alicia used a handful of these to eliminate roughly 20% of

her workload. Report generation, client updates, routine email responses—gone. Not delegated to a person, but offloaded to a machine.

And this isn't just anecdotal. A recent McKinsey study found that automating predictable tasks can increase productivity by up to 30% in knowledge-based roles.

CALENDAR AND MEETING OPTIMIZATION

Meetings consume time. Poorly managed meetings devour it.

Today's leaders spend an average of 23 hours a week in meetings—many of which could've been an email, a Slack update, or better yet, avoided altogether. Calendar optimization tools help reduce the friction and reclaim focused time.

- **Calendly** – Allows others to book time based on your real-time availability. (Note: Motion.ai also integrates this feature.)
- **Clockwise** – Protects deep work blocks and dynamically adjusts your calendar to avoid conflicts.
- **Fellow.app** – Helps you run better meetings with shared agendas, note tracking, and follow-up reminders.

By defining when, why, and how she met with others, Alicia gained back five hours per week. No more interruptions during peak focus time. No more last-minute calendar scrambles. Just deliberate, structured time that aligned with her priorities.

MANAGING EMAIL WITHOUT GETTING LOST IN IT

Email, once a marvel of modern communication, now behaves more like a relentless toddler—constantly demanding attention. Leaders spend an average of 28% of their workweek in email. The cost isn't just time—it's cognitive fragmentation.

AI-powered filters and batching strategies help bring order to the chaos:

- **SaneBox** – Shuffles unimportant emails into a "Later" folder so your main inbox stays clean.
- **SpamSieve & Hey.com** – Act as intelligent gatekeepers, screening emails before they hit your inbox.
- **Boomerang** – Schedules emails and follow-ups at optimal times for better timing and fewer distractions.

Alicia, once glued to her inbox for nearly three hours a day, now checks email twice—once mid-morning and once late afternoon. By combining batching, automation, and prioritization, she slashed her email time by over 75%.

Worth repeating is something we called attention to in Chapter 3: researchers at UC Irvine found it takes over 23 minutes to fully refocus after checking email. Even five "quick glances" a day can quietly drain two hours of productivity.

CHOOSING THE RIGHT APPS WITHOUT OVERLOAD

Sometimes, the productivity problem is the productivity tool.

More apps mean more tabs, more passwords, more updates—and more context switching. Each jump burns focus, increases friction, and fragments your day.

As you optimize your tech stack, ask these questions of each app:

- Does the tool automate a repetitive task?
- Reduce cognitive effort?
- Integrate with your existing workflow?

If the answer is no, it's probably friction dressed up as innovation.

Alicia dropped five tools after doing a tech audit. She consolidated her task and meeting management into Motion. ai, which also handled booking. She adopted SaneBox for email filtering. Her new stack was leaner, clearer, and less mentally taxing.

BEST PRACTICES FOR AUTOMATION

Technology works best when it supports structured habits. Random automation is like a Roomba in a forest—technically moving, but not accomplishing much.

Here's A flight plan I recommend:

1. **Automate the Right Tasks**
   Not everything should be automated. Repetitive, rule-based tasks are ideal. Human judgment still wins in creativity, nuance, and empathy.

2. Create Conditional Workflows
   If a task happens more than three times a week, it's a candidate for automation.

Examples:

- If an email contains "invoice," route it to accounting.
- If a meeting is booked, reserve 30 minutes beforehand for prep.
- If a report is finalized, auto-send it to the team.

3. Use Templates for Common Tasks
   Prewritten replies, document formats, and email scripts reduce friction. Even a few saved minutes per task add up to hours per month.

4. Set Up Digital Boundaries
   Use tools like Freedom to mute notifications and Noisli for ambient focus.

   Also worth noting: Dr. Andrew Huberman, a Stanford neuroscientist, frequently explores how 40 Hz gamma wave stimulation can enhance cognitive functions like focus, concentration, and problem-solving (this is a personal productivity hack I use daily.) His lab's research into brainwave entrainment (utilizing 40 Hz binaural beats) suggests this stimulation can sharpen attention—and even improve mood.

5. Review Quarterly
   Automation isn't "set and forget." Quarterly reviews keep your system lean. Alicia found this shift so valuable she made tech reviews a quarterly habit: if a tool didn't save time, it was cut.

CREATING A SEAMLESS DIGITAL ECOSYSTEM

It's not about having the fanciest tech—it's about harmony.

Your tech stack should function like a symphony: distinct tools playing in sync, without stepping on each other.
Alicia's final setup looked like this:

- SaneBox + Boomerang – Email triage and smart follow-ups
- Motion.ai – Task prioritization and calendar protection
- Zapier – Seamless automation across platforms
- Noisli + Spotify/40 Hz Gamma Waves – Ambient focus and brainwave entrainment

Every tool served a purpose. None operated in isolation. The result? A workflow that felt smooth, intuitive, and increasingly second-nature.

THE ROI OF A WELL-DESIGNED TECH SYSTEM

Time mastery doesn't mean working faster. It means working smarter—with intention, clarity, and flow.

Alicia began overwhelmed, reactive, and digitally overcommitted. Within three months, her schedule was lean, her mind was clear, and her results spoke for themselves.

Technology didn't make her superhuman. It simply cleared the runway so she could take off.

And that's the promise: Not more hours—more ownership.

CALIBRATION QUESTIONS

1. Which digital tools in my current workflow are creating more friction than freedom?
   → *Helps me pinpoint tech that's slowing me down instead of speeding me up.*

2. When was the last time I reviewed my productivity tools for actual effectiveness?
   → *Reveals whether my tools are still serving me—or just taking up space.*

3. Am I automating repetitive tasks… or just enduring them out of habit?
   → *Encourages me to identify missed opportunities for time-saving systems.*

4. How often do I mistake being digitally busy for being truly productive?

→ *Prompts me to distinguish between activity and meaningful progress.*

5. How well is my current tech setup protecting space for deep, focused work?

→ *Encourages me to evaluate whether my tools are safeguarding what matters—or just adding noise.*

6. Does my tech stack function like a cohesive system—or a noisy collection of apps?

→ *Helps me assess whether my tools are working together or working against each other.*

7. What's one small shift in my digital habits that could return a big-time dividend?
   → *Invites low-effort, high-impact thinking for immediate improvement.*

_____

_____

_____

_____

"A smart tool should make you feel smarter. If not—lose it."

RECOMMENDED RESOURCES

1. **Deep Work** by Cal Newport
This book emphasizes the importance of deep, focused work in a world filled with distraction. It aligns closely with the chapter's emphasis on minimizing digital noise and creating environments for high-impact productivity. Readers will walk away with practical strategies for building sustained focus and protecting their cognitive energy.

2. **Make Time** by Jake Knapp & John Zeratsky
A highly actionable guide that teaches readers how to design each day with intention. The book encourages creating systems and boundaries around time—many of which are supported by technology. It's a helpful companion to this chapter's themes of purposefully shaping your digital environment.

3. **Digital Minimalism** by Cal Newport
Newport argues that cluttered digital lives reduce our capacity for meaningful work and joy. His framework for reducing tech dependency aligns well with creating a streamlined, efficient digital ecosystem. This is an excellent next read for anyone feeling buried under the weight of too many apps or notifications.

4. **Getting Things Done** by David Allen (Podcast + Book)
A classic in productivity literature, GTD offers practical systems for organizing tasks and commitments. The emphasis on trusted systems and reduced mental clutter supports this chapter's message of offloading tasks to technology. Both the podcast and book help readers develop personal accountability with structured workflows.

5. **The Tim Ferriss Show** (Podcast)
    Tim's long-form interviews frequently spotlight leaders who optimize their time and workflow using innovative tools. This podcast serves as an idea farm for new systems, tech hacks, and productivity philosophies. It supports the principle of continual system improvement and iteration.

6. **Work Clean** by Dan Charnas
    Applying a chef's mise-en-place philosophy to knowledge work, this book helps professionals design thoughtful, repeatable workflows. It aligns with the themes of automation, task batching, and structure. Charnas' ideas offer a fresh perspective on preparation and flow in a high-demand environment.

7. **Productivityist** (Blog + Podcast by Mike Vardy)
    Focused on intentional time use, Vardy's work blends mindset, technology, and methodology. His discussions on digital boundaries and thoughtful tool integration echo many of the strategies in this chapter. A go-to resource for those wanting to level up how they use productivity apps.

8. **The Focused Podcast** by David Sparks & Mike Schmitz
    A podcast devoted to maintaining focus in a digitally distracted world. The hosts regularly dive into tool selection, automation, and routine design—all foundational topics in this chapter. Their personal examples make complex systems relatable and practical.

9. **Tools of Titans** by Tim Ferriss
    A treasure trove of habits, tools, and techniques from world-class performers. Many of the interviewees share how they leverage technology to buy back time and stay focused. It's a goldmine for readers looking to experiment with new systems.

10. Ali Abdaal (YouTube Channel)
Abdaal offers deep dives into productivity tools, personal operating systems, and time-saving strategies. His tutorials are especially helpful for tech-curious professionals looking to streamline workflow. The visual walkthroughs make implementation far less intimidating.

11. Superhuman Blog
Dedicated to the science of email productivity, this blog offers tactics that complement the chapter's approach to managing inbox overload. Topics range from cognitive science to software use—all geared toward saving time and improving digital hygiene. It's especially useful for those ready to optimize communication flow.

12. Zapier Blog
A hub for exploring the power of automation through practical case studies and tutorials. This resource helps demystify workflows across apps, aligning directly with this chapter's sections on automation. It's perfect for readers wanting to build their first—or fiftieth—automated system.

15 | THE CLOCKWISE CULTURE
DEVELOPING A TEAM THAT RESPECTS TIME

"TIME DOESN'T DISAPPEAR. IT GETS BORROWED, INTERRUPTED, OR HIJACKED—USUALLY BY SOMEONE WITH GOOD INTENTIONS AND A SLACK ACCOUNT."

– JASON FRIED –

Co-founder and CEO of Basecamp

THE DISRUPTION TAX: HIDDEN COSTS OF CASUAL INTERRUPTIONS

Raj never imagined that something as invisible as time would become the most misused asset in his company.

Not his own time—he'd been managing that well enough. But his team's time. Or more specifically, how casually they expected it from one another.

It showed up in small ways. A five-minute chat that turned into thirty. A "quick favor" that derailed someone's afternoon. Slack messages tossed like tennis balls into a dozen conversations without regard for whether someone was in the middle of deep work or even available. Questions asked in the name of collaboration that could have waited—or never needed asking in the first place.

At first, Raj dismissed it as just the normal noise of a growing team. "This is what agility looks like," he told himself. But over time, he noticed something deeper: frustration simmering beneath the surface. People showing up late to real priorities because their day had been carved up by the needs of others. Projects that should have flown getting bogged down not by poor strategy—but by a thousand barely visible interruptions.

One afternoon, after a particularly inefficient group huddle that felt more like a therapy session than a tactical meeting, Raj pulled his department heads aside. Not to scold—but to ask a question.

"How much time," he asked, "do you think we cost each other in a week... simply by not respecting one another's focus?"

They blinked. No one had really thought about it like that.

So, Raj did what Raj does—he pulled out a whiteboard and started drawing boxes.

"Let's say you interrupt someone for just 10 minutes, twice a day. And let's assume they lose another 10–15 minutes each time trying to refocus. Multiply that by five days, then by 8 team members, and you've burned through nearly 20 collective hours a week just from small, well-intentioned interruptions."

He turned and wrote one word at the top of the board:

MUDA — the Japanese term for waste.

That moment shifted the room. The problem wasn't laziness. It wasn't incompetence. It was culture. A culture where time was seen as flexible—especially other people's time. And like most culture problems, it hadn't been designed that way. It had simply been allowed.

Raj realized they didn't need stricter policies—they needed deeper values. The kind that respect people's focus as much as their feelings. Values that treat someone's calendar like their concentration zone, not public domain. Values that understand the hidden cost of one "harmless" interruption is often the quiet erosion of productivity and excellence.

Over the following weeks, Raj led his team through a subtle but powerful redesign. Not of tools—but of trust. They created shared norms around how and when to ask for someone's time. They started using non-interruptive communication where possible. They began checking calendars before dropping requests.

Perhaps most importantly, they started asking a simple but game-changing question: *"Is this worth the interruption?"*

It didn't eliminate all inefficiency. But it did shift something foundational: a mutual sense of respect. A collective awareness that the way we treat time—especially each other's—says something about what we truly value.

And for the first time in a long time, Raj wasn't the only one guarding the team's momentum.

TIME DOESN'T WORK IN ISOLATION

Time doesn't work in isolation—and neither do people. One small disruption rarely stays small. It triggers a chain reaction that ripples quietly through an organization, showing up as missed deadlines, delayed decisions, and fractured focus. What begins as one person asking for "just a minute" often ends in someone else working late to recover the hour they lost.

Raj began to see this clearly. A quick check-in with a teammate in the hallway delayed a client proposal. That delay bumped a review meeting. That meeting, pushed into someone else's deep work block, disrupted their flow—and pushed the real work into after-hours. One small interruption. Four disrupted schedules. None of it malicious. All of it costly.

And it's not just anecdotal. We already know that there's more to consider than just the interruption, there's also the focus recovery time afterward. Stack just a few of those in a day, and you've drained a workweek before Wednesday.

What's worse—teams often normalize it. Leaders mistake responsiveness for engagement. Employees reward immediacy over intentionality. And somewhere along the line, a culture forms where everyone feels busy, but no one feels effective.

This is the quiet erosion of alignment. Leaders set meetings without clarifying objectives. Team members reply to emails at midnight, unintentionally signaling that availability equals value. Deadlines become flexible. Priorities drift. And a slow fog of disorganization settles over the team—not because they lack talent, but because they lack *shared time values.*

High-performing teams look different. They trade chaos for clarity. They communicate with purpose. They build-in guardrails that protect focus. They rely on tools and updates that don't require everyone to stop what they're doing in order to preserve momentum. And perhaps most importantly, they respect each other's time as if it were their own.

Raj didn't need to hire more people. He didn't need productivity hacks. What his team needed was a shared time ethic. A shift from individual urgency to collective awareness. And once that shift began, time stopped slipping through the cracks. It started flowing in the same direction.

DESIGNING A CULTURE THAT RESPECTS TIME

Raj didn't fix his team's time challenges by handing out productivity apps or sending a strongly worded email about efficiency. He fixed it by reshaping the culture. One conversation, one shift, one shared value at a time.

Here's how he did it—and how you can too.

1. **Create Guardrails for Communication**
   The first shift Raj made wasn't technical—it was emotional. He called a meeting and told his team:

   "We're not doing each other any favors by being constantly available."

   They talked openly about the pressure to respond right away. The feeling of always being "on." The guilt that crept in when someone didn't reply to a Slack message fast enough—even if they were deep in client work or in the middle of a project that required real thought.

So, they set guardrails. Not rigid rules—but shared expectations:

- **Urgent issues?** Call or drop by.
  If something was truly time-sensitive—client fire, system outage, blocked deliverable—it warranted a direct phone call or a walk to someone's desk. No guessing. No delay.
- **Same-day needs?** Send a message.
  For items that needed action before the day was out, a Slack message or direct ping was fine—but it had to be clear, concise, and respectful of the other person's workflow.
- **Regular updates?** Email by end of day.
  Routine updates, status checks, and FYIs were gathered and sent via email, ideally in a single digest, giving the recipient space to respond without pressure.
- **Non-urgent items?** Drop them in a weekly review doc.
  Ideas, questions, and low-priority items went into a shared document reviewed once a week—ensuring they were captured without interrupting anyone's flow in the moment.

The effect was immediate. People checked their inboxes with intention instead of anxiety. Focus time increased. Response guilt decreased.

2. **Reclaim Focus with Time-Protection Rituals**
   Next, Raj helped the team protect their deepest work from their noisiest habits. They picked one morning a week—Wednesday—to be meeting-free and message-light. Phones on silent. Calendars blocked. No pings. No dings.

One engineer said it was the first time she'd been able to finish a complex deliverable in a single uninterrupted block in over a year.

They also began scheduling "Focus Sprints"—protected 90-minute windows, two or three times a week, marked clearly on everyone's shared calendar. During those blocks, distractions were treated like open flames. People learned to honor them. Productivity climbed.

The result wasn't just better work. It was quieter work. Calmer work.

3. Shift from Interruption to Intention

Raj introduced a simple challenge to the team: "Before you send that message or schedule that meeting—ask yourself: Can this wait? Can this be clearer? Can this be shorter?"

They started using recorded video updates in Slack instead of dragging five people into a live call. They summarized decisions in shared docs rather than rehashing them in a new thread. They logged tasks in their project tracker—then trusted the system to notify the right people.

Slowly, the need to "just check in real quick" began to disappear. In its place came margin—space to think, space to create, space to breathe. And when real-time collaboration was needed? They set "office hours"—open windows when team members could bring questions or solve obstacles together. It wasn't about being unavailable. It was about being intentional.

4. **Clarify Decision-Making Authority**
So much wasted time hides behind unclear ownership.
Decisions stall. Questions float. Meetings multiply. Raj saw
it happening all the time—two people assuming someone
else was making the call. Like Milton Friedman once said,
""when everybody owns something, nobody owns it."

So, he implemented a dead-simple decision map:

- **Owner: Makes the call.**
This is the person responsible for the final decision. They
gather input if needed, but they're empowered to move
forward without waiting for consensus.
- **Advisor: Offers input.**
Advisors contribute expertise or perspective. They're
consulted early—but they don't hold veto power and aren't
looped into every update.
- **Informed: Kept in the loop, but doesn't weigh in.**
These are stakeholders who need visibility but not
involvement. They're notified of decisions after the fact so
they stay aligned without slowing things down.

That alone slashed unnecessary meetings by 20%. Projects
stopped bouncing between inboxes. And team members
felt the shift—less "checking in," more moving forward.

5. **Build Accountability Through Visibility**
Raj knew that clarity wasn't a one-time event—it had to be
baked into the workflow. So, the team picked a handful of
tools and stuck with them.

Tasks went into one tracker. Updates lived in one channel.
Ownership was clearly marked. No more wondering who
was doing what. No more chasing updates.

But Raj added one more piece: they measured progress together. Not just performance metrics, but cultural signals—evidence that their time was being used well and wisely. Every month, the team reviewed a few simple but telling indicators:

- **How much time was spent in meetings?**
  They tracked the actual hours on the calendar and compared them against outcomes. If time spent didn't match value delivered, it signaled the need to trim, restructure, or eliminate.
- **How many tasks hit deadlines?**
  Missed deadlines weren't punished—but they were explored. If a pattern emerged, it often pointed to overloaded schedules, unclear ownership, or competing priorities.
- **Were team members feeling energized—or stretched thin?**
  They checked in on how people were actually doing—not just what they were producing. Burnout, overwhelm, or constant catch-up mode meant something in the system needed adjusting.

That feedback loop kept the team honest. And it turned abstract values—like "respect for time"—into something practical, visible, and deeply human.

THE RIPPLE EFFECT OF A TIME-RESPECTING CULTURE

The shifts Raj's team made didn't make headlines. There were no sweeping memos or slick new platforms rolled out. No bold declarations. Just quiet decisions, repeated daily, rooted in a simple conviction:

Everyone's time matters.

And once that conviction took hold, it was reflected in how they communicated, collaborated, and honored each other's schedules.

As a whole they moved through their days with a sense that their time—and their attention—was finally being treated like a resource, not a renewable one.

CALIBRATION QUESTIONS

1. What unspoken habits or norms in my team are quietly devaluing one another's time?
   → *Helps me surface cultural blind spots that may be sabotaging productivity or trust.*

2. When I ask for someone's time—do I treat it as a transaction or a trust?
   → *Encourages me to examine my mindset around collaboration and respect.*

3. What signals am I sending—intentionally or not—about availability, urgency, and responsiveness?
→ *Prompts me to consider how my behavior sets the tone for the whole team.*

4. How clear is my team on when they're expected to be responsive—and when it's okay to protect their focus?
→ *Invites me to evaluate whether we've defined (and defended) healthy boundaries.*

6. Where are decisions in our team getting delayed simply because roles, ownership, or authority aren't clearly defined?
→ *Encourages me to identify the places where clarity could accelerate progress.*

7. What would it look like to create a culture where protecting someone's time was seen as an act of leadership, not isolation?
   → *Inspires a reframe: that time stewardship is not a solo act, but a shared value.*

> *The more you plan with purpose, the less you apologize with regret.*

FINAL THOUGHTS

Creating a time-conscious team isn't about squeezing more out of people—it's about giving them the conditions to do their best work without burning out in the process.

When time is honored, people feel valued. When structure shows up, chaos quiets down. When the culture starts pulling in the same direction, momentum builds without the usual friction.

It doesn't take a grand overhaul. Just a series of small, intentional steps—led with clarity, reinforced with care.

And if you start there, your team won't just thank you. They'll follow you

RECOMMENDED RESOURCES

1. **Essentialism** by Greg McKeown
This book is a manifesto for doing less, but better. It explores the high cost of saying yes to everything—and how undisciplined activity can create unintentional waste across teams. It reinforces the idea that respecting other people's time starts with sharpening our own priorities.

2. **The Power of a Positive No** by William Ury
Ury's book teaches leaders how to set healthy boundaries without damaging relationships. It's a vital companion for teams learning how to protect their focus, say no with clarity, and resist the pressure of constant availability. It aligns beautifully with Raj's shift toward intentional communication norms.

3. **Work Clean** by Dan Charnas
Adapted from the world of professional kitchens, this book introduces the concept of mise-en-place as a system for mental clarity and structured work. It offers practical strategies for time-blocking, preparation, and reducing decision fatigue—making it a natural fit for teams that want to streamline collaboration and respect each other's margin.

4. **It Doesn't Have to Be Crazy at Work** by Jason Fried & David Heinemeier Hansson This modern classic challenges hustle culture and offers a vision for a calm, focused workplace. It's packed with real-world tactics for reducing unnecessary communication, avoiding meetings by default, and building respectful time practices into team operations. It supports nearly every cultural shift Raj's team made.

5. **Team of Teams** by General Stanley McChrystal
   McChrystal's leadership framework focuses on decentralizing decision-making and increasing clarity of roles across teams. It highlights the importance of alignment, autonomy, and trust—all critical themes in a culture that values time and minimizes bottlenecks. A strong companion to the "Owner / Advisor / Informed" model introduced in this chapter.

6. **Time Smart** by Ashley Whillans
   Based on Harvard research, this book explores how we often trade time for money in unwise ways—and how to reverse that pattern. It provides a compelling business case for treating time as a scarce resource and aligning teams around habits that protect it. It echoes Raj's focus on shared guardrails and cultural clarity.

7. **The Culture Code** by Daniel Coyle
   Coyle dives deep into how high-performing cultures are built through safety, vulnerability, and shared purpose. It provides insight into how subtle norms—like how teams use each other's time—signal deeper values. An excellent match for readers who want to go beyond systems and into the emotional intelligence of leadership.

8. **The Focus Course Podcast** by Shawn Blanc
   This podcast offers short, thoughtful episodes on focus, digital minimalism, and personal productivity—many of which directly apply to team leadership. It reinforces the idea that attention is worth protecting and that intentional rhythms create healthier output. A strong supplement to the chapter's conversation around deep work.

9. **Brave New Work** by Aaron Dignan
   Dignan explores the invisible operating systems that govern how teams work—often unconsciously. His framework for redesigning team behaviors aligns with Raj's cultural audit and the ripple effects of time-awareness in organizations. It's a bold yet practical guide for leaders who want to initiate change from the inside out.

10. **Managing for Focus** (Harvard Business Review article)
    This article offers research-backed insights into how leaders can reduce fragmentation and distraction in their teams. It speaks directly to the cognitive costs of casual interruptions and the need for focus-enabling leadership. It's a great primer for building the business case behind many of this chapter's strategies.

11. **Deep Work** by Cal Newport
    No list on time-respect and focus would be complete without this foundational work. Newport lays out the cognitive science behind distraction and offers tangible steps for creating meaningful focus—individually and across teams. It strongly supports the deep work blocks and interruption-limiting practices Raj implemented.

12. **The Long and the Short of It Podcast** by Adam Morgan & Mark Barden
    This podcast from the creators of "A Beautiful Constraint" explores how teams can do more with less—time, resources, energy—without sacrificing creativity. It pairs well with the chapter's message that limitation can actually produce clarity and momentum. Ideal for readers looking to sustain the cultural shifts they've begun.

TIME GAMBIT

16 | AGENCY IN THE FIRST HOUR

THE LEADER'S EDGE

"YESTERDAY IS GONE. TOMORROW HAS NOT YET COME. WE HAVE ONLY TODAY. LET US BEGIN."

– MOTHER TERESA –

RUNNING HARD. STARTING WRONG

Ethan paced his office, frustration simmering beneath the surface. His day had unraveled before it even began. A late-night email had sparked an issue that all but guaranteed a good night's sleep would be a vain pursuit—and it still lingered into the morning. A client had escalated a minor complaint, and his assistant, thinking she was being helpful, rescheduled a critical meeting during the first hour of the workday without checking with him first. Consequently, everything got pushed back—including an important strategy session that had now been bumped for the second time. By noon, Ethan deflated into his office chair, coming to terms with the fact that his real work—the kind that actually moved the company forward—hadn't even been started.

This wasn't unusual.

For years, Ethan wore his nonstop availability like a badge of honor. Long hours and constant responsiveness, he believed, were the marks of a committed leader. He prided himself on jumping into every fire and solving problems in real time. But living in reactive mode for so long left him completely spent by day's end. Weekends fell short of the margin he needed to recharge, and the coming week always arrived faster than recovery. Motivation gave way to survival.

Then came the moment that quietly disrupted everything.

It wasn't a dramatic event—just a passing comment from a mentor over coffee. But the words landed with unexpected weight, lodging in Ethan's brain like a splinter he couldn't ignore:

"Your first hour decides the next ten."

Ethan scoffed, half-laughing as he raised an eyebrow. "That sounds like something from a motivational poster," he said. "Mornings don't matter anymore than the rest of the day. I'm working every minute I'm awake."

His mentor didn't flinch. He just sipped his coffee and replied calmly, "I'm not asking you to believe it. I'm asking you to test it. For one week, start your day on your terms. No phone. No email. No outside noise. Just you, your mind, and your mission. Own the first hour."

Ethan didn't buy it—but something in the tone, the conviction, or maybe just the fatigue in his own soul nudged him to try.

And that one week? It rewrote the rhythm of his life.

He didn't become a morning monk or start running ultra-marathons before sunrise. But he carved out space—just one hour—where he was in charge. No screens. Ten minutes of silence. A short workout. A clear priority list. Then, and only then, did he open the floodgates of his day.

His energy improved. His thinking sharpened. The chaos didn't vanish, but it no longer dictated his day. He stopped reacting and started leading.

The shift wasn't in how much he worked—it was in how he began.

WHY MORNINGS SHAPE THE WORKDAY

Most leaders wake up and immediately plug into the world. Emails. Notifications. Headlines. Urgencies. Their mental mode is forced to shift instantly to a reactive state before their brain has had time to adjust—before what's referred to as sleep inertia has had a chance to shake off. The science backs this up. Optimal cognitive performance is impossible because physiological changes such as cerebral blood flow take time to occur. According to a study by Harvard Health, automatic responses are triggered putting you into fight or flight, a condition that should be reserved for real emergency conditions.

THE MECHANICS OF FIGHT OR FLIGHT

The fight or flight response at the core of our brain is a survival mechanism. During times of increased stress, the liver and pancreas will dump enormous amounts of sugar and insulin into the bloodstream as a response to the emergency. Today, the stresses we face do not allow us to use the excess sugar and insulin. There is no outlet, so the hormone cortisol stores it. Since fat is inherently inflammatory, it triggers more internal physiological stress.

Worry is a stress that your body cannot differentiate between what will actually happen and what we think may happen. So even when the stress is not real, emotional stress occurs. The process of worry is the same whether large or small. We project what may happen in the future and assess whether or not we have the resources needed to cope with anticipated outcomes. Worry is another survival mechanism. Properly placed, it's useful. Worrying about how to survive an approaching hurricane and preparing for it is properly placed. We can forecast with some accuracy what we may soon need. Worry about how quickly we need to answer emails is not.

Scientists have found that low-grade chronic inflammation in those as young as 18-20 affected cognitive ability, so you're not doing yourself any favors by being "on top of everything" first thing in the morning. Recovery from fight or flight can take weeks or months. When it's chronic, you're heading for disaster.

With a few bad experiences in our history, we may get into the habit of always predicting bad outcomes. This is called catastrophic thinking. We anticipate catastrophes from even normal everyday events. To prepare for these awful events we initiate the fight or flight response.

Learned helplessness is a passive reaction to situations we can't control or think we can't control. So, we engage catastrophic thinking in an attempt to control every situation.

If this sounds familiar, the world has already handed you its agenda before you've had a chance to think about setting a direction for your day.

This matters more than we like to admit—because how a leader starts determines how they steer. We can learn to train our brains so that our natural reactions are a healthy response.

When you launch your day with intention—calm, focused, deliberate—you carry that posture forward. But when the day begins in chaos, you're not likely to emerge from it.

A consistent morning routine becomes an anchor. It creates psychological safety before the unpredictable waves of leadership demands begin to crash in.

Science affirms what seasoned leaders intuitively know. Studies published in the Journal of Applied Psychology suggest that structured morning routines reduce decision fatigue and improve emotional regulation throughout the day. Another study from Harvard Business Review found that executives who began their days with reflective time reported a 23% increase in perceived productivity compared to those who didn't.

Ethan's turnaround wasn't about waking up earlier. It was about reclaiming sovereignty over his time.

MORNING AND EVENING ROUTINES: BOOKENDS THAT BUILD RESILIENCE

Leadership invites a thousand demands per day. If you don't design your rhythm, someone else will. That's why structured morning and evening rituals are essential. They serve as bookends—establishing boundaries that protect your energy, focus, and well-being.

Think of it like building a mental fence around the things that matter most.

1. **Morning Routines (The First 60 Minutes): A Strategic Launch**
   Great leaders don't stumble into their day. They step into it intentionally.

   Essential components of a high-impact morning routine:

- No screens for the first 30 minutes. Email and news hijack your attention before priorities are even set. Let the world wait.
- Movement to activate energy. A short walk, light stretch, or simple workout jumpstarts focus and releases endorphins.
- Intentional stillness. Prayer, meditation, journaling, or breathwork calms the soul and primes the mind.
- Clear priorities. Identify the three things that matter most. Not the inbox. Not the fire drills. The essentials.

   Ethan's new rhythm followed this flow: ten minutes of stillness, light movement, a simple breakfast, and a prioritized task list. He didn't check his phone until he had established clarity on his own terms.

The result? He no longer felt like his mornings were being stolen from him.

2. Evening Routines: The Night Before Matters
How you finish today shapes how you begin tomorrow.

Leaders who resist the urge to "catch up" late at night often wake with greater clarity and better rest. Evening rituals help the mind release tension, reflect on the day, and reset for what's next.

Elements of an effective evening ritual:

- Set a shutdown time. Know when the workday ends—and guard it like it matters. Because it does.
- Reflect. What worked? What didn't? What needs your attention tomorrow? (Limit this to seven items—max.)
- Preview the next day. Identify your top three objectives. This removes the morning guesswork.

- Digital sunset. Powering down devices improves sleep and protects your mental bandwidth. Employ the *"Amish Hour"*: all screens off one hour before sleep time.
- Ethan was skeptical. He used to spend his evenings trying to "get ahead." But in truth, he was grinding down his edge. When he introduced a digital sunset at 8:30 p.m. and added a brief journaling habit, his sleep improved—and his mind was clearer at dawn.

THE RIPPLE EFFECT OF STRUCTURE

Ethan's transformation wasn't a result of Herculean discipline. He didn't wake up at 4:00 a.m. to climb mountains and meditate in a cave. He simply took control of the first and last frames of his day.

The ROI?

- Clarity. He began each day with his true priorities front and center.
- Calm. He no longer felt ambushed by urgency.
- Energy. He slept better, thought clearer, and made better decisions.
- Progress. Strategic work got done. Every. Single. Day.

A FEW FAMOUS TEMPLATES

You don't need to mimic others, but it helps to learn from them. High performers across industries craft their days with intention.

- Tim Cook (Apple): Starts at 4:00 a.m., reviews select emails, then hits the gym before facing the day.
- Jocko Willink (Former Navy SEAL & Author): Wakes daily at 4:30 a.m., hits the gym immediately, and posts his sweaty watch face on social media to remind the world that discipline equals freedom.
- Jeff Bezos (Amazon): Shields his mornings from meetings and uses them for deep, strategic thinking.
- Tim Ferriss (Author & Investor): Mixes meditation, journaling, and movement in the first hour—testing rituals

constantly to find what creates clarity and creative flow.
- Simone Biles (Olympic Gymnast): Structures her mornings around fuel, focus, and form—with carefully timed meals, stretching, and mental rehearsals.

Each approach is unique. But the principle is the same: Start with design, not demand.

SIMPLE TEMPLATES YOU CAN MAKE YOUR OWN

Morning (60 Minutes):

- 5 Minutes – Wake up without screens
- 10 Minutes – Physical movement
- 10 Minutes – Stillness or reflection
- 10 Minutes – Planning top priorities
- 10 Minutes – Reading or journaling
- 15 Minutes – Preparing (breakfast, calendar review)

Evening (30 Minutes):

- 10 Minutes – Reflect on the day
- 10 Minutes – Identify tomorrow's top seven
- 10 Minutes – Wind-down to Digital Sunset

It's not the length of time. It's the intention behind it.

A Word of Caution (with a Wink)

If you've ever tried to build a morning routine and failed by DAY 2, welcome to the human race! We've all had that "This is the new me!" moment that faded as quickly as the smell of fresh coffee. Don't start by aiming for perfection. Start by showing up.

One leader I coached tried to overhaul his entire morning routine in one day. He started journaling, meditating, cold plunging, intermittent fasting, and reading Stoic philosophy— all before 6:00 a.m. He lasted three days and needed a nap that lasted half a weekend.

Consistency over complexity. That's the game.

CALIBRATION QUESTIONS

1. What is currently shaping the first 60 minutes of my day— intention or interruption?
   → *Prompts reflection on whether I'm owning my morning or letting it be hijacked.*

2. How do I typically feel by mid-morning, and what does that reveal about my current routine?

→ *Helps me connect my energy levels to the way I start my day.*

3. In what ways does my evening routine support—or sabotage — my next day's success?

→ *Challenges me to see how tonight's habits echo into tomorrow's clarity.*

4. What specific habits could I implement this week to protect my morning clarity?

→ *Invites small, actionable steps that anchor my first hour.*

5. When was the last time I felt truly in control of my day from the start? What was different then?
   → *Encourages a look back to rediscover patterns that worked.*

6. How might my leadership effectiveness improve if my day began with clarity instead of chaos?
   → *Stretches my imagination to consider the upside of intentional rhythms.*

7. Who in my circle models a healthy start to their day, and what could I learn from them?
   → *Prompts me to study real-life examples that could inspire my own practice.*

> *Clarity isn't found in your inbox.*
> *It's built before you open it.*

FINAL THOUGHTS

Leadership is too important to leave to chance—and so is the way you begin your day. The first hour doesn't just set the tone; it establishes the terms. It's where priorities are clarified, distractions are held at bay, and ownership begins.

Time is one of the few resources you can never earn back. Each morning offers you a gift—and a responsibility.

> *How you begin reflects what you value. And what you value gets built into the bones of your leadership.*

You don't need a perfect routine. You need a faithful one. Not flashy. Not complicated. Just consistent—anchored in purpose and protected with resolve.

Agency isn't found in the chaos. It's built in the quiet. Before the meetings. Before the messages. Before the mayhem.

Steward your first hour like it matters–because it does.

Start where it counts: the beginning.

One hour of intention can change the next ten—and, over time, change everything.

RECOMMENDED RESOURCES

1. **The Miracle Morning** by Hal Elrod
   This book offers a compelling framework for designing a structured morning that fuels energy, clarity, and productivity. Elrod's SAVERS model—Silence, Affirmation, Visualization, Exercise, Reading, Scribing— provides a simple but powerful set of rituals to anchor your day. His story-driven approach makes the practice both inspiring and accessible for high-capacity leaders.

2. **Make Time** by Jake Knapp and John Zeratsky
   This practical guide helps readers take back control of their daily rhythm by focusing on one meaningful highlight per day. It blends behavioral science with real-world application, offering actionable strategies for starting each day with clarity and intentionality. Particularly relevant are their insights on building "daily anchors" that resist the pull of constant urgency.

3. **Lead Yourself First** by Raymond M. Kethledge and Michael S. Erwin
   This book explores the power of solitude and reflection in leadership—practices that are often most accessible during the morning hours. Through historical case studies, the authors show how leaders have harnessed quiet, focused time to make better decisions and cultivate resilience. It's a thoughtful companion for anyone seeking to reclaim their internal clarity before facing external demands.

4. **Triggers** by Marshall Goldsmith
   Goldsmith unpacks how our environment and daily rituals shape our behavior, often more than we realize. He offers a set of tools for becoming more conscious of the triggers that either propel us forward or pull us off course. It's especially helpful for leaders trying to break reactive patterns and build intentional routines.

5. **The Power of When** by Dr. Michael Breus
   This science-backed exploration of chronotypes helps readers align daily tasks—including morning and evening rituals—with their biological rhythms. Breus introduces four distinct types and shows how syncing with your natural energy peaks can improve productivity, sleep, and mood. It's a great resource for customizing the timing of your routines for maximum impact.

6. **High Performance Habits** by Brendon Burchard
   Burchard presents six key habits that consistently correlate with long-term success, drawing from extensive research and coaching experience. Morning clarity and evening resets are core themes throughout the book, emphasizing the importance of strategic bookends to each day. For leaders seeking a blend of motivation, science, and structure, this delivers.

7. **The Daily Stoic** by Ryan Holiday
   A collection of 366 daily reflections based on Stoic philosophy, this book is ideal for grounding the mind in wisdom and perspective before the day begins. Each entry is short, meditative, and paired with commentary that helps apply the ancient principles to modern leadership. A perfect tool for anchoring morning stillness or journaling rituals.

8. **The Craig Groeschel Leadership Podcast**
    This faith-based podcast blends personal discipline with leadership insight, often highlighting the invisible routines that create visible results. Episodes frequently emphasize the importance of morning intentionality, margin, and building systems that shape sustainable impact. It's a practical and encouraging resource for value-driven leaders.

9. **Michael Hyatt's Blog**
    Hyatt's blog archives are rich with insights on productivity, goal-setting, and the power of structured daily rhythms. He consistently advocates for morning rituals, digital boundaries, and planning systems that align with your priorities. His work is especially helpful for entrepreneurs and executives looking to lead from rest, not reactivity.

10. **The 5 AM Club** by Robin Sharma
    This book challenges readers to rise early and use the first hour of the day for personal mastery. Sharma weaves storytelling with strategy, offering a 20/20/20 formula (movement, reflection, learning) that mirrors many elements of this chapter. While the tone is motivational, the framework is actionable for leaders looking to reclaim their mornings.

11. **Rest: Why You Get More Done When You Work Less** by Alex
    Soojung-Kim Pang
    This book flips the script on productivity by making a case for structured rest and daily rhythm. Pang draws from neuroscience, history, and real-world research to show how leaders who prioritize deliberate breaks and routines

outperform those who grind without margin. His insights align perfectly with the case for morning and evening bookends.

12. The Art of the Start 2.0 by Guy Kawasaki
While positioned as a startup guide, this book delivers high-impact routines and mental frameworks for anyone launching a new initiative—including your day. Kawasaki's emphasis on clarity, focus, and energy management aligns well with this chapter's call to reclaim the first hour. His direct, irreverent tone makes the advice stick.

17 | IN THE EYE OF THE STORM
WHAT CRISES TEACH US ABOUT TIME

> ## "YOU CAN'T STOP THE WAVES, BUT YOU CAN LEARN TO SURF."

– JON KABAT-ZINN –

*Professor of Medicine emeritus
University of Massachusetts Medical School*

THE STRONGEST MOVE WAS STEADINESS

It was one of those break-point moments—the kind you never forget.

Dillon was in production management at a commercial printing company when they landed a major account with a nationwide brand. Big name. Big expectations.

Big opportunity.

The first project was already on the presses—a sleek print piece designed by an outside agency, high-volume, full-color, and destined for stakeholders across the country.

Everyone on the team felt the weight of it. This job wasn't just ink and paper. It was a foot in the door, and nobody wanted to be the reason it slammed shut.

Then came the call.

There was an error. A visible one. It had made its way into the first batch of samples sent to the agency.

The problem had originated on Dillon's end—inside the plant. One of those mistakes that slips past every checkpoint because everyone assumes someone upstream surely would have caught it. But no one had.

By the time it was discovered, the damage was done. Samples had already been sent—including a set to corporate headquarters. The tone of the client's voicemail said it all: this wasn't just about the error. This was about whether they could trust Dillon's team.

And just to twist the knife, the job had already burned through premium stock, expensive inks, billable press time, and labor. A reprint would carve deep into already razor-thin margins.

The old Dillon would've gone full scramble mode—racing from department to department, barking orders, crashing meetings, and firing off emails in a frenzy to regain control.

But not this time.

Instead, he walked quietly to his office, closed the door, silenced his phone, and set it face down on the desk. Then he walked to the whiteboard.

What happened next revealed more about Dillon's leadership than the job ever could. He didn't dodge. He didn't deflect. He didn't look for someone to blame.

He owned it—fully. Calmly. Confidently.

At the top of the whiteboard, he wrote two questions:

- What matters most right now?
- What can wait?

In that pause, he found what urgency and crisis often try to hide—clarity. This wasn't just about fixing a print run. It was about preserving a relationship, a reputation, and a culture of accountability.

He jotted down four clear priorities:

- Call the client directly to take ownership and steady the conversation.
- Reassure the internal team—panic would only amplify the problem.
- Correct the error and resume the run with focus.
- Launch a swift root-cause review to prevent it from happening again.

Moments later, his assistant walked in with a stack of meeting requests others had already started scheduling. Dillon looked up—calm, deliberate.

"Cancel all non-essentials," he said. "I'll speak with the client myself—then with the team."

He stood, straightened his posture, and walked into the next conversation—not with fear, but with focus. He wasn't losing control. He was learning to lead through it.

They reset, re-ran the spoiled portion, ate the cost, and still delivered on time. The agency never left.

That moment of crisis—when the pressure was on and a lesser leader might've tried to disappear—became a turning point. Not because the work was flawless, but because the response was.

Dillon learned something that day: In high-stakes moments, it's not just your performance that earns trust—it's your posture.

> *How you respond when things go wrong speaks louder than how you perform when it all goes right.*

HOW TO MANAGE UNEXPECTED DISRUPTIONS

Crises pull back the curtain and expose every flaw, every inefficiency, every shaky assumption about how time should be managed. When the problems spike and uncertainty dominates, weak leaders panic. With their minds caught in a damage control loop, they try to do it all. They drown in activity but accomplish little. Author Simon Sinek got it right, "Leadership isn't tested in the calm, it's revealed in chaos."

Exceptional leaders operate differently. They don't speed up, they slow down—intentionally, courageously. They focus on the few things that matter, stay grounded when others spiral, then move with strategic calm.

> *A scattered leader builds a scattered team.*

PAUSE BEFORE REACTING

Our first instinct during a crisis? Move! Do something. Anything. But motion without a clear plan burns valuable time and resources.

Instead, effective leaders pause. Not for long, but long enough. Enough to recalibrate, prioritize, and stop reacting to emotionally charged noise around the situation.

They:

- Step away from the flood of input sources—emails, texts, calls—and step into clarity.
- Write a short, prioritized list of objectives that will define their focus.
- Ask: What most effects long-term impact? Not what feels loudest, but what lasts longest.

Dillon didn't rush into meetings. He created space for himself to think. That moment created margin, and that margin created clarity.

TRIAGE THE CRISIS

Not every problem deserves your time equally.

Crises often feel like a tsunami of equal-sized waves. But in reality, they break down into three categories:

- **Category 1: Immediate Actions** – These are pressure points. If ignored, they amplify the problem. These demand the leader's presence.
- **Category 2: Delegated Issues** – Still important, but solvable by others. Assign them.
- **Category 3: Lower-Priority Tasks** – These can wait, but will likely need attention later. Some might actually resolve themselves.

Dillon zeroed in on Category 1: public messaging, internal stability, and strategic oversight. Everything else? He handed it off or let it go.

PROTECT DECISION-MAKING ENERGY

Crises drain the mind. The sheer number of decisions, questions, and variables can wear down even the sharpest thinker.

The wise leader intentionally protects their cognitive bandwidth.

How?

- **Eliminate trivial decisions:** These are items that likely fall in Triage Category 3. Outsource or simplify them.
- **Batch similar decisions:** Handle like-issues in one focused session with stakeholders.
- **Take brief mental resets:** A walk, a quiet space, even five minutes of deep breathing can help you recalibrate.

Dillon didn't read every email. He didn't attend every call. He filtered. He conserved his time and sharpest thinking for his highest priorities.

STRATEGIES FOR MAINTAINING FOCUS UNDER PRESSURE

In a crisis, distractions don't disappear... they multiply and amplify. People want answers. Stakeholders demand reassurance. Information arrives faster than it can be processed.

A leader who can focus amid that noise is a rare asset.

CREATE A CONTROLLED INFORMATION FLOW

Too much information is as dangerous as too little. The key is to control the stream.

- Appoint a gatekeeper: Someone you trust who filters updates.
- Set communication windows: Check messages at fixed intervals, not constantly.
- Use brief summaries: Bullet-pointed updates. This is faster, clearer, and easier for your team to absorb and recall.

Dillon's assistant distilled updates hourly. He stayed informed, but not overwhelmed.

ENFORCE PRIORITY BLOCKS

Emergencies beg for your time and attention, but not all attention is productive.

- Block off time for strategic thinking: In a crisis, uninterrupted space is vital.
- Protect boundaries: Make it clear when you're not available.
- Explain your tactic: Let key players know that you're not avoiding, you are formulating your response to the crisis. Ask them to protect your space for a few minutes and tell them how long you need. Over time they will begin to understand that this is how you roll in similar scenarios. Emerge with a plan.
- Reduce live meetings: Not every update needs a Zoom call. Asynchronous updates can be faster.

Dillon carved out thirty sacred minutes. No interruptions. Just thinking, planning, choosing.

USE STRATEGIC DELEGATION

Delegation is not abdication. It's precision.

- Identify talent: Match tasks to people who can own them.
- Clarify objectives: Vague asks waste time. Be specific.
- Trust and verify: Empower, don't hover.

Dillon handed communication with production teams to key team leaders and technical investigation to customer service and prepress managers. No micromanaging. Just alignment.

IMPLEMENT A RAPID DECISION FRAMEWORK

In a crisis, paralysis is costly. Define how you will respond when (not if) a crisis arises. Here's a quick decision-making model:

1. Clarify and articulate the issue
2. List possible responses
3. Assess risk vs. reward
4. Make the call and act quickly

Dillon used this exact framework to authorize a voluntary recall. The risk of and uncertain way-forward and delayed response to the design agency outweighed the cost of transparency.

CONTROL EMOTIONAL RESPONSES

"Stress doesn't make us stupid; it makes us short-sighted." - Martha Beck

Emotional regulation is an unspoken superpower of effective crisis leadership.

- Breathe before speaking: Even a short pause helps.
- Anchor in facts: Choose truth over fear.
- Project calm: Teams take emotional cues from the top.

Dillon exuded steadiness. That steadiness became contagious.

RECALIBRATE PLANS IN REAL TIME

Few plans survive contact with a live crisis. That's not a flaw. It's reality. The best leaders adapt without losing direction.

- Know the final outcome you are pursuing (the pathway that takes you there is subject to change)
- Scan for new data frequently
- Quickly recalibrate strategies with the desired outcome
- Communicate updates clearly with stakeholders (internal and external alike)

Dillon updated his team as new info came in. By day's end, the plan had developed, and his team stayed in lockstep.

WHY THIS SHOULD MATTER

When crisis hits, most leaders go into overdrive. But the ones who endure—the ones who actually gain ground in the chaos—aren't the loudest or the fastest. They're the ones who can hold their nerve, regulate their emotions, and make calm decisions in turbulent moments.

And it's not just theory.

Study after study confirms the same pattern: leaders who stay composed under pressure don't just survive the crisis—they earn trust, elevate performance, and build stronger teams in the process.

In a multi-year study from the Center for Creative Leadership, executives who ranked high in crisis resilience led companies that saw:

- 24% higher employee retention, and
- 29% greater investor confidence over five years.

The takeaway?

Clear-headed leadership in high-stakes moments doesn't just protect the business—it strengthens it.

It creates confidence, loyalty, and long-term momentum that no spreadsheet can fully measure.

MASTERING TIME IN THE STORM

Dillon didn't escape the crisis. He led through it. He didn't dodge the fallout or magically prevent the consequences. He made time work for him—in spite of the pressure swirling around him. He wasn't superhuman. He was just anchored. Anchored in a mindset. Anchored in a method. Anchored in a posture that refused to let panic set the pace.

He chose:

- Clarity over chaos.
- Intentional pause over impulsive reaction.
- Trust over control.
- Frameworks over guesswork.

When combined, that formula made all the difference. Because when the storm hits—and it surely will—it's not how fast you move that defines your leadership.

It's whether moves you make actually matter.

And that brings us to you.

What happens when your plan gets hijacked? When crisis crashes your calendar and time seems to vanish beneath the urgency?

The next section is designed to help you establish the gap— between how you typically respond, and the kind of leadership response that brings real stability in unstable moments.

Let's take inventory.

CALIBRATION QUESTIONS

1. How do I typically respond when unexpected problems disrupt my schedule?
→ *Helps me recognize instinctive reactions and how they shape the early minutes of a crisis.*

2. What signals tell me I'm reacting instead of responding?
→ *Prompts awareness of physical, emotional, and behavioral cues that signal reactivity.*

3. Have I identified which tasks only I can do during a crisis, and which can be delegated?
→ *Encourages clarity on role boundaries, delegation, and energy protection under pressure.*

4. Do I have a structured approach for making high-stakes decisions quickly?
→ *Surfaces the presence (or absence) of a repeatable decision-making process.*

5. How do I manage my emotions under pressure, and what impact does that have on my team?
   → *Connects emotional regulation to leadership influence and team trust.*

6. Who filters information for me when the flow becomes overwhelming?
   → *Highlights the value of a gatekeeper or system to protect decision-making bandwidth.*

7. What disciplines or habits help me stay centered in the storm?
   → *Points to practical rhythms that anchor clarity, courage, and presence in real time.*

> *In a storm, it's not your speed that saves you— it's your steadiness.*

FINAL THOUGHTS

You don't get to choose the timing. But you do get to choose the response.

That's the defining edge of resilient leadership.

Because the wrong response doesn't just cost composure— it costs time. Panic multiplies problems. Reactivity creates rework. And when a leader spirals, so does the team—burning energy, focus, and resources that are already in short supply.

The leaders who navigate crisis well don't do it with bravado. They do it with clarity, steadiness, and trust. They don't outrun the chaos. They remain grounded inside it. They slow the spin. They protect what matters. They create margin to think when others are scrambling to act. They know which conversations need their full presence, which decisions demand their sharpest attention, and which tasks can—and should—be released to others.

That's how time is preserved in a storm: not by controlling everything, but by choosing what matters most, and moving only with intention. As James Lane Allen once wrote, "Adversity does not build character—it reveals it." Crisis doesn't crown leaders. It unmasks them.

And in that moment—when time, trust, and tension all hang in the balance—what will your posture reveal?

RECOMMENDED RESOURCES

1. **Leadership in Turbulent Times** by Doris Kearns Goodwin
   Goodwin offers a compelling look into how Lincoln, Roosevelt (Teddy and Franklin), and Lyndon Johnson led the nation through periods of intense upheaval. The book illustrates the mindset and behaviors that define calm, principled leadership under pressure. It affirms the idea that composure and courage—more than charisma—make the difference in crisis.

2. **The Obstacle Is the Way** by Ryan Holiday
   Holiday draws from ancient Stoic wisdom to present a philosophy of endurance, perspective, and purpose in the face of adversity. His tactical approach to mindset reframing shows how crisis can become a path to mastery rather than a detour from it. It reinforces the chapter's call to lead with grounded resolve rather than reactive emotion.

3. **Dare to Lead** by Brené Brown (Book + Podcast)
   Brown's work explores the intersection of vulnerability, trust, and courage in leadership, especially when stakes are high. She provides language and tools to stay emotionally present while navigating tough decisions. Her insights directly support the chapter's section on emotional regulation as a leadership multiplier during crisis.

4. **Your Brain at Work** by David Rock
   This neuroscience-based guide explains how to manage attention, energy, and decision-making in high-pressure environments. Rock's model helps leaders understand how to prevent cognitive overload and stay strategic when

time is tight. It pairs seamlessly with the chapter's section on protecting decision-making energy and limiting input fatigue.

5. **The Look & Sound of Leadership with Tom Henschel** (Podcast)
   Executive coach Tom Henschel delivers short, practical lessons on communication, presence, and influence in the boardroom and beyond. His episodes are especially valuable for leaders working to maintain steady, credible communication during chaotic moments. The podcast reinforces the chapter's theme of leading through posture and tone—not panic.

6. **Multipliers** by Liz Wiseman
   Wiseman shows how the most effective leaders get more from their teams not by doing more themselves, but by drawing out the full potential of others. Her framework teaches how to delegate with precision and avoid becoming the bottleneck in a crisis. It strongly supports the chapter's emphasis on empowered delegation during moments of high demand.

7. **Harvard Business Review's On Emotional Intelligence**
   This collection of essays dives deep into the foundational role of emotional awareness and regulation in leadership. It offers research-backed strategies for staying calm, connected, and constructive in the face of disruption. The essays echo and expand on this chapter's theme that emotional steadiness is not optional—it's a leadership differentiator.

8. **The Coaching Habit** by Michael Bungay Stanier
   This book teaches leaders how to ask better questions instead of defaulting to advice or control. It encourages a coaching posture that builds clarity, ownership, and autonomy within teams—even under time pressure. It complements this chapter's discussion of posture and reinforces the idea that strong leaders create space for others to rise.

9. **WorkLife with Adam Grant** (Podcast)
   Organizational psychologist Adam Grant interviews leaders and thinkers on how to build healthy, resilient, high-performing workplaces. Many episodes address crisis navigation, emotional stamina, and leading with curiosity instead of control. His work aligns with the chapter's challenge to stay centered and adaptive under pressure.

10. **Radical Candor** by Kim Scott
    Scott provides a framework for clear, kind, and direct communication—especially vital when the stakes are high and time is limited. Her approach helps leaders navigate tough conversations without sacrificing connection or clarity. It reinforces the idea that calm transparency can stabilize a team faster than a flood of updates or mixed signals.

11. **Thinking in Bets** by Annie Duke
    Former poker champion Annie Duke reframes decision-making through the lens of probability and risk management. She shows leaders how to act with speed and confidence even when certainty is impossible. This directly supports the chapter's rapid-decision framework and encourages smarter, faster calls when every minute counts.

12. **Decision Leadership** by Don Moore & Max Bazerman
    Moore and Bazerman explore how leaders can shape the
    decision environments of their teams for better long-term
    outcomes. Their framework highlights the ripple effect of
    leadership clarity in high-stakes scenarios. This resource
    echoes the chapter's emphasis on proactive structures and
    filters to manage chaos without letting it manage you.

18 | WHAT GETS MEASURED GETS MASTERED

MEASURING AND IMPROVING OVER TIME

"YOU MUST NEVER CONFUSE FAITH THAT YOU WILL PREVAIL IN THE END — WHICH YOU CAN NEVER AFFORD TO LOSE — WITH THE DISCIPLINE TO CONFRONT THE MOST BRUTAL FACTS OF YOUR CURRENT REALITY, WHATEVER THEY MIGHT BE."

- ADMIRAL JAMES B. STOCKDALE -

United States Navy aviator

THE ATHLETE WHO TRACKED HIS WAY TO SUCCESS

Derek had once been the kind of man who could shave fractions of a second off a race time just by adjusting the angle of his saddle or fine-tuning his sleep schedule. As a professional cyclist, precision wasn't a preference—it was survival. Every ride was logged. Every metric tracked. He knew his power output the way most people know their own birthdays. Cadence, hydration, heart rate, recovery time—if it moved the needle, he measured it.

And when he won, it wasn't because he pushed harder. It was because he optimized better.

So, when Derek hung up his helmet and transitioned into the world of consulting, he assumed that same athlete's edge would carry over. At least, that's what he told himself.

But business, he quickly learned, was a different kind of race.

His calendar resembled a mosaic of obligations, beautiful from a distance but impossible to navigate up close. His inbox would often spawn a second inbox by mid-morning. Strategy—his supposed strong suit—was wedged into the cracks between client calls and administrative clutter. He was moving fast, no doubt. But toward what? That part was harder to pin down.

One late night, somewhere between brushing his teeth and climbing into bed, Derek paused at the bathroom mirror and asked the question every high-achiever eventually stumbles into:

"Am I actually winning... or just surviving?"

His first instinct was to set his alarm an hour earlier. Just one more hour, he reasoned. One more hour to claw back control. But then, like a headwind hitting hard on a steep climb, another thought cut through:

"In sports, I measured everything that mattered. Why am I flying blind now?"

It was the mental gear shift he didn't know he needed—until that moment.

Instead of starting earlier, he started smarter. Derek launched a full-scale time study on himself. He tracked when his energy peaked and when it flatlined. He sorted his week by categories: deep work, shallow work, distractions. He treated his calendar like race footage—studying every move, searching for wasted motion.

The truth surfaced quickly. Forty percent of his week was disappearing into meetings. Another twenty percent: email and text quicksand. The work that actually moved the needle—his strategic output—was left fighting for the scraps.

Armed with the data, Derek did what any elite athlete would do: he adjusted. Aggressively.

Meetings were confined to narrow windows on specific days. Email checks became scheduled, timed, and trimmed. Mornings—his peak performance zone—became sacred ground for creative and strategic work. Afternoons were reserved for the reactive stuff. He stopped chasing productivity and started designing it.

Six months later, Derek had recovered—or repurposed—over ten hours a week. Revenue climbed. Blood pressure didn't. He wasn't scrambling anymore. He was steering.

The breakthrough wasn't another productivity hack. It wasn't brute force.

It was clarity.

And it started the moment he stopped guessing and started measuring.

WHY MEASURING MATTERS—IN BUSINESS AND BEYOND

Derek's story isn't just a nod to personal clarity. It underscores a universal principle: *you can't improve what you don't measure.*

And this isn't just a personal productivity insight—it's a proven business advantage.

A 2022 Harvard Business Review study found that organizations with a clear habit of measuring key performance indicators (KPIs) across departments were 2.5 times more likely to outperform their peers in revenue growth and profitability. Companies that regularly reviewed time allocation, goal progress, and operational metrics made faster decisions, recovered quicker from missteps, and reported higher employee engagement.

Meanwhile, research from McKinsey & Company confirmed that businesses using real-time data to track performance and adapt strategy were over 60% more likely to achieve above-average financial returns than those relying on intuition or legacy systems.

In other words, measurement isn't bureaucracy—it's clarity in motion.

Where gut instinct leaves room for bias, measurement brings objectivity. Where winging it feels fast, measuring reveals whether you're actually gaining ground.

And that's true whether you're leading a team of two or two hundred.

HOW TO EVALUATE YOUR TIME MANAGEMENT PROGRESS

Most professionals assume they're using time well. But assumptions come with blinders.

Real insight requires measurement. Just like a fitness tracker reveals how sedentary your day really was, time tracking pulls back the curtain on your habits. The best leaders don't guess where their time goes—they measure it. They study patterns. Then they make intentional, data-informed shifts.

Derek didn't stumble into productivity. He brought the rigor of elite training to his calendar.

Step 1: Track Your Time with Brutal Honesty

Start with a detailed log. And don't sugarcoat it. Most professionals underestimate how much time gets lost to low-value tasks.

Take a lawyer who bills 60 hours a week—yet only 30 of those go toward actual casework. Or a manager booked in back-to-back meetings all week, making meaningful decisions in just five of those hours.

Tracking kills self-deception.
Choose your method:

- **Manual Logging** – Write down activities in 15-minute increments. A spreadsheet works fine. So does an old-school notebook.
- **Time Tracking Apps** – Tools like RescueTime, Toggl, or Clockify automate the process, categorizing your digital

behaviors and revealing where your attention actually went.

- **Calendar Review** – At the end of the day, log time spent on each meeting or task. Identify how many hours truly moved the needle.

When Derek finally tracked his day, he discovered email was eating three hours daily. He had assumed it was thirty minutes. Whoops.

Step 2: Categorize Work by Value

Not every task deserves a starring role. Just because your day was full doesn't mean it was fruitful.

One of the most dangerous traps for high-capacity professionals is mistaking *movement for momentum.* We've been conditioned to celebrate packed calendars, but the truth is—busyness isn't the same as effectiveness.

To reclaim your time, start by classifying your work into three simple categories:

- **Deep Work** – The kind that matters most. This includes strategic thinking, creative problem-solving, focused writing, planning, or any task requiring sustained mental presence that drives meaningful results. Done well, deep work shifts the trajectory of a project—or your career.

- **Shallow Work** – Necessary, but not transformative. These are the logistical, administrative, and coordination tasks—

emails, scheduling, status updates.

Shallow work is loud and persistent, but rarely produces breakthroughs. The key is to contain it, not eliminate it.

- **Distractions** – These are the time-thieves that pose as productivity: unnecessary meetings, compulsive inbox checking, mindless scrolling, reactive firefighting. They may feel urgent, but they rarely serve your highest goals. Learning to spot and sideline them is a discipline that pays dividends.

When Derek saw that only 20% of his time was spent in deep work, it triggered a complete restructure.

The result? A shift from scattered effort to focused, intentional output.

Step 3: Identify Constraints

Once you start tracking, constraints (or bottlenecks) leap out at you—like plot holes in a B-movie.

Watch for common culprits:

- Meetings without a clear purpose or outcome
- Email overload and the notification distraction loop
- Low-priority tasks stealing time from peak-performance hours
- A lack of structured focus time for deep work

Derek's biggest constraint? Endless client meetings with no guardrails. He started limiting calls to designated time blocks. It was like giving his calendar a digital enema.

KEY METRICS AND REFLECTION PRACTICES

The goal isn't more hours worked; it's more productivity during the hours worked.

There are four core key metrics that shift the focus from effort to effectiveness. Each one gives you a diagnostic lens to refine how your time is actually spent.

- **Time-to-Task Ratio**
  This metric separates activity from impact. It asks: How much of my time is actually devoted to work that moves the mission forward? By calculating the percentage of your week spent on high-value, outcome-driving tasks versus low-value or maintenance work, you gain visibility into your alignment. If the ratio's skewed, that's a red flag—too much energy is being poured into the shallow end of the pool.

- **Energy Mapping**
  Not all hours are created equal. Energy mapping helps you identify your personal peak-performance windows—the stretches of time when your mind is sharp, your creativity is high, and your execution is fast. Once you know those zones, you can prioritize deep work during those hours and save lighter tasks for your energy valleys. It's about syncing your schedule with your biology instead of

forcing productivity uphill. This builds directly on the principles we explored in Chapter 10—where we learned that managing your energy, not just your time, is the true unlock for sustainable performance.

- **Decision Fatigue Indicators**
  Every decision costs mental energy—and eventually, the quality of those decisions starts to slip. This metric invites you to track how many meaningful choices you're making in a day and when your decision-making starts to dull. Spotting the signs early allows you to front-load key decisions, build in recovery, and offload routine choices through systems, habits, or delegation.

- **Meeting Efficiency Score**
  Not all meetings are bad—but far too many are pointless. This score evaluates whether your meetings consistently produce clear decisions, next steps, or meaningful outcomes. A full calendar isn't the win; clarity and action are. A high score signals alignment. A low score? That's your cue to trim, reframe, or cut entirely. We hit this head-on back in Chapter 2: "Meeting Overload." This metric brings that chapter's insights into real-time practice—helping you separate calendar clutter from true forward motion.

Derek's energy map showed peak focus from 7:00 AM to 11:00 AM. So, he redesigned his mornings for strategy and creativity—saving emails and calls for the afternoon slog.

Reflection transforms that data into insight. Each of the following practices helps you convert raw information into wiser decisions and sharper priorities. Just like a coach doesn't watch game film to admire what happened—but to improve what happens next—your reflection practices help you refine your rhythm, catch drift early, and keep your time aligned with your priorities.

- **Weekly Review**
  Once a week, step back and examine how your time was truly spent—not how you hoped it would be. Ask: Was I intentional or reactive? Did I prioritize what mattered, or did I just respond to what was loudest? This isn't about guilt—it's about *recalibration.* A short review gives you the chance to spot leaks, realign focus, and walk into the next week with sharper clarity.

- **Monthly Optimization**
  Every 30 days, identify one inefficiency and address it directly. Maybe it's a recurring meeting that no longer delivers value. Maybe it's a clunky tool or a cluttered morning routine. The goal isn't to overhaul everything— it's to prune deliberately. Because small, consistent improvements add up. And over time, they compound

- **Quarterly Reset**
  Every 90 days or so, life shifts—and your systems should, too. This reset invites you to revisit your routines, commitments, and assumptions. Are your habits still serving your long-term goals? Are you operating from vision or just momentum? A quarterly reset isn't about scrapping everything—it's about recalibrating the compass before you drift too far off course.

After just one month, Derek's deep work time increased by 30%. Not bad for a guy who used to spend half his day stuck in inbox purgatory.

THE POWER OF CONTINUOUS TRACKING AND REFINEMENT

Time management isn't a one-and-done solution. It's a process—one that lives and breathes.

Don't try to do everything at once.
Do the right thing next.

Sustainable improvement doesn't come from dramatic overhauls. It comes from consistent calibration. High performers don't wait for burnout to force change. They build habits of steady refinement that keep their systems sharp, their minds clear, and their calendars responsive. Here are a few practices that create a rhythm for ongoing excellence:

- **The 1% Rule:** Aim to improve just one small thing each week—a process, a routine, a boundary, or a decision-making habit. Over time, those micro-upgrades compound like interest. One percent might not feel like much today, but string together fifty-two of them, and a year from now, you'll be operating at an entirely different level—without the chaos that comes from reactive, stop-and-start change.
- **Eliminate One Task Monthly:** Every month, identify a

task that no longer serves the mission. Maybe it's something that could be delegated to someone better suited, automated with a tool, or eliminated altogether because its relevance has expired. Trimming just one unnecessary obligation each month clears space for higher-value work—and sends a clear message to your calendar (and your team): only what's essential gets to stay.

- **Adjust Quarterly:** Life doesn't stand still. Priorities evolve. Roles shift. What worked six months ago might be slowing you down now. A quarterly adjustment gives you the opportunity to reassess your workflow, refit your tools, and realign your routines with what matters most in the current season. It's not about chasing perfection. It's about staying agile and aligned.

Derek didn't stop measuring once he got things "right." He kept reviewing his data. He kept making micro-tweaks. And over time, those gains added up—just like compound interest.

Want proof?

Another Harvard Business Review study from 2021 found that professionals who tracked their time and reviewed it weekly reported a 23% increase in task completion rates, along with significantly lower stress levels.

Turns out, owning your time really does make a difference.

CALIBRATION QUESTIONS

1. What am I currently measuring about how I use my time—
   and what am I still guessing at?
   → *Pushes me to confront the gap between intuition and actual data.*

2. What did I learn the last time I tracked my time, and how
   did it change my behavior?
   → *Encourages reflection on how past measurement impacted decision-making.*

3. Which part of my weekly routine feels efficient—but
   hasn't actually been measured for effectiveness?
   → *Exposes hidden inefficiencies that may be hiding behind familiarity.*

4. What's the one metric that would most help me evaluate whether my time is well spent?
→ *Invites clarity around what really matters—and how to track it.*

5. How much of my calendar reflects intentional design versus reactive obligation?
→ *Encourages measurement of alignment, not just activity.*

6. What patterns would I see if I reviewed how much deep work I actually do each week?
→ *Prompts honest assessment of how much time is spent on meaningful, high-impact work.*

7. If I tracked my time for just one week, what behaviors or
    routines do I suspect would surprise me?
    → *Invites curiosity and reveals where blind spots might be hiding.*

> *The difference between motion and momentum is measurement.*

FINAL THOUGHTS

The gap between burnout and breakthrough isn't talent. It's
awareness. And awareness begins with measurement.

When you measure your time, you don't just understand it
better—you start to own it. You move from drifting to directing.
From reacting to redesigning.

Data doesn't lie and it doesn't apologize. It doesn't care how
busy your week felt. It simply shows you the truth: where your
time actually went, and what it cost you.

Derek's transformation wasn't about hustle. It was about
stewardship. He didn't work more hours—he worked smarter
within them.

> *When you track what matters, you stop wasting what you can't afford to lose.*

Here's the paradox: Measuring your time doesn't cost you time—it shows you where you're losing it so you can get it back.

You identify the leaks. You catch the drift. You clear out the noise. And in the process, you recover hours you thought were gone for good.

Mastery isn't born in the big moves. It's forged in the small measurements that, when taken seriously, compound into freedom.

The leaders who consistently measure don't just optimize. They align. They reclaim. They lead on purpose.

The freedom we're after doesn't live in chaos. It lives in quiet clarity. And clarity begins the moment we stop guessing—and start measuring.

RECOMMENDED RESOURCES

1. **The Deadline Effect** by Christopher Cox
   Cox explores how consciously applying pressure—by setting clear deadlines—magnifies focus and efficiency. It mirrors Chapter 18's insight that measurement (in this case, time-bound constraints) can sharpen execution and reduce drift. If you want to harness time rather than let it wash over you, this book demonstrates that structured urgency creates clarity.

2. **Slow Productivity** by Cal Newport
   Newport advocates against the constant hustle, emphasizing how incremental, measured progress beats frantic bursts. His philosophy aligns with the chapter's 1% Rule and continuous calibration: small, tracked adjustments lead to sustainable performance. It reinforces that mastery is built not by chaos, but by thoughtful measurement.

3. **Organize Tomorrow Today** by Jason Selk & Tom Bartow
   This book recommends a nightly habit: planning tomorrow with specific metrics (wins, blocks, behaviors) that then get reviewed the next day. It dovetails with this chapter's advice on weekly and monthly reflection, turning measurement into a habit rather than a chore. Readers learn to anchor productivity in routine, data-informed practice.

4. **Four Thousand Weeks** by Oliver Burkeman
   Burkeman offers a philosophical yet practical lens on time's finite nature, urging us to measure our commitments with intention. His framing reinforces the chapter's stewardship theme: measurement isn't about more—it's about meaningful presence. It's a grounding companion

to the idea that data helps us align time with what truly matters.

5. **Accelerate** by Nicole Forsgren, Jez Humble & Gene Kim
    Based on extensive research, this book shows how measurable metrics—like deployment frequency and lead time—drive high-performing teams and cultures. It reinforces the chapter's message that what gets measured gets improved, at both individual and systemic levels. Its data-driven approach to performance mirrors the time-measurement mindset we champion here.

6. **Measure What Matters** by John Doerr
    Doerr's introduction to the OKR framework underscores the power of defining clear metrics, tracking them consistently, and adapting based on outcomes. This mirrors the chapter's core coaching steps: track, review, refine— then repeat. It reminds readers that clarity and alignment arise from measurable accountability.

7. **My Fixation on Time Management Almost Broke Me** by Abbie J. Shipp (Harvard Business Review)
    Shipp shares a candid account of obsessing over time tracking to the point of burnout, then learning to recalibrate with reflection and boundaries. The story echoes Chapter 18's tip: measurement without reflection can backfire— and recalibration is key. It makes the case that data must lead to awareness, not more busyness.

8. **Time Management Is About More Than Life Hacks** by Erich C. Dierdorff (Harvard Business Review)
    Dierdorff's piece reminds leaders that time management is a decision-making discipline—not a collection of tricks. It aligns with the chapter's framing that measurement

isn't a hack, it's a habit that allows for strategic flexibility. The article reinforces that real time mastery comes from proactive structure, not reactive fixes.

9. **Why We Need to Take a Data-Driven Approach to Measuring Productivity** by Forbes Tech Council
The article showcases how organizations that establish clear, measurable metrics for productivity outperform those that rely on anecdote. It reinforces Chapter 18's case from the organizational level: true time stewardship begins with objective data. The piece bridges individual habits and broader time-management cultures.

10. **Time Audit Guide** (Timeneye Blog)
This practical guide walks readers through a rigorous time-audit process—track, analyze, adjust—complete with templates and next-step recommendations. It's a hands-on match to Derek's journey and the chapter's framework, helping readers translate concept into action. This guide ensures that readers don't just measure—they also iterate and optimize.

11. **Time Tracking – Will it Make You More Productive?** (Paperless Movement Podcast)
In this episode, hosts discuss real-world examples of time tracking revealing hidden inefficiencies—like prep time, context switching, and tooling delays. Their analysis echoes the chapter's Energy Mapping and Time-to-Task Ratio sections, showing how reflection leads to structural improvements. It's a practical reinforcement of the idea that you can't fix what you don't measure.

12. **Beyond Productivity: How Businesses Can Measure and Act on What Matters** by Forbes Business Council
This article invites leaders to expand time-based measurement into broader performance indicators—customer satisfaction, resolution times, and value creation. It supports Chapter 18's invitation to think beyond hours logged—to the quality and impact of those hours. The argument resonates with the chapter's final call: measurement isn't cynicism, it's stewardship.

19 | TURNING TIME INTO MOMENTUM
FROM VISION TO ACTION

"VISION WITHOUT ACTION IS A DAYDREAM. ACTION WITHOUT VISION IS A NIGHTMARE."

– JAPANESE PROVERB –

THE MOMENT URGENCY LOST ITS GRIP

Elliot sat at the head of a long walnut conference table, empty coffee cups scattered around like trophies from battles he didn't recall winning. His team had just left—the last of them offering a tight smile before retreating to yet another crisis-in-progress. The whiteboard behind him looked like a mish-mash of half-erased scribbles: deadlines, issues, customer complaints. The word launch was circled three times in red, as if urgency alone could will the service into existence.

The week had been brutal. A key investor was breathing down his neck for results. Sales had dipped. His customer support team was drowning in unresolved tickets. And that morning, they learned a rival startup had undercut their pricing—so aggressively that it made Elliot's jaw tighten. His marketing director proposed a fire sale to keep from losing more ground.

And twisting the knife was his CFO who raised valid concerns about quarterly cash flow.

Elliot—the founder who once thrived on chaos—suddenly felt like a pinball ricocheting from one flashing light to another.

Later that day, over a previously scheduled lunch with one of his business mentors, Elliot candidly unpacked how he'd felt after the team meeting, sparing no detail. Just when he should have felt some relief from unloading the mental weight, a simple question came back across the table:

"Where do you see the company in ten years, Elliot?"

He blinked. A ten-year plan? Awkwardly, he had to admit he didn't really have one—at least not one he could articulate with any clarity. He had quarterly goals. A one-year revenue target. Maybe a vague sense of where things should go. But a real, vivid picture of the future? Nothing could have felt more elusive in that moment.

His mentor sat quietly for a beat, then leaned in with the kind of calm that comes from decades of scars and stories.

"That's not unusual," he said. "But it is dangerous. If you don't define the destination, chaos will be glad to do it for you."

Elliot stared down at his untouched plate.

"Let me ask it another way," the mentor continued. "What would make all this worth it? The stress. The sacrifice. The time away from your family and friends. If you woke up ten years from now and nothing had changed except your revenue... would that be enough?"

It hit like a brick wrapped in velvet.

Until that moment, Elliot had believed speed was his superpower. But now, it felt more like drift.

That question—and the silence that followed—reset his internal compass in a way nothing else had. Elliot realized he wasn't leading a company. He was managing a series of reactions. The rival startup wasn't playing the same game. They were playing chess while he'd been playing checkers.

His mentor, sensing that Elliot's hardened soil was finally being tilled by this new awareness, seized the moment to revisit a subject they'd danced around before—but now, it was time to bring it home.

"You've always understood the value of setting clear goals for yourself and your team," his mentor affirmed. "But what I'm talking about is more than that. Without a clear vision for your company's future state, your organization is like a ship without a rudder—or worse, without any compass heading at all. No one could predict where that vessel would land... there are far too many variables."

The metaphor drew a slow, silent nod from Elliot.

His mentor continued. "Let's revisit what I mean when I talk about vision and goals:

Vision is about the why and the where. It's a vivid picture of your preferred future—capturing both the destination and the deeper purpose behind the journey. Vision is directional, emotionally compelling, and usually not tied to a specific timeframe. It inspires action and provides clarity amid complexity. Think of it as the North Star: fixed, guiding, and above the noise.

Goals, on the other hand, are about the what and the when. What will you need to do and when in order to make your vision a reality. They're the measurable mile markers lining the road toward the vision. Goals are time-bound, often quantifiable, and help you assess progress. They don't replace vision—they serve it. Think of goals as the stepping stones that bring vision within reach, one intentional step at a time."

Elliot knew in that moment: this was the missing element. The recalibration he needed.

BALANCING SHORT-TERM DEMANDS WITH LONG-TERM GOALS

Every leader feels the grind. The morning inbox. The urgent phone call. The product glitch that couldn't have come at a worse time. These demands pull you into the current, creating the illusion of progress while quietly robbing you of direction.

Organizations that chase urgency often sacrifice strategy. They pivot too quickly. They burn through talent. They throw marketing dollars at symptoms instead of systems. And the cost? Long-term sustainability.

Here are a few signs your team might be stuck in the short-term trap:

- **Constantly shifting priorities to respond to the latest fire.**
  When urgency dictates your agenda, strategy loses traction. The team becomes reactive—constantly starting

over instead of building momentum. Long-term goals get sidelined, and alignment with the broader vision starts to fade.

- **Decisions made on emotion or instinct instead of data or strategy.**
  Knee-jerk reactions may feel decisive, but they often create confusion and inconsistency. Without a guiding framework, leadership becomes unpredictable, and your team is left guessing.
  Emphasis on near-term revenue at the expense of long-term positioning. Quick wins—flash sales, rushed launches, short-term promos—can feel productive. But over time, they chip away at brand equity, erode trust, and trade tomorrow's traction for today's dopamine hit.
- **Rising burnout among high performers due to perpetual urgency.**
  Talented team members are expected to sprint endlessly without clarity, margin, or recovery. Morale tanks, turnover climbs, and institutional knowledge walks out the door.

Leaders who win with time know how to zoom out. They understand that short-term wins might feel gratifying, but lasting success is built on the slow, deliberate layering of systems, culture, and vision. This is how traction takes hold—not in the sprint, but in the steady cadence of intentional steps that compound over time.

Making time work for you means resisting *the tyranny of the urgent* long enough to invest in what matters most. Because when you stop reacting and start building, time stops slipping away—and starts working in your favor.

THE CHESS MASTER'S APPROACH TO TIMING

A chess master doesn't just respond to an opponent's move. They anticipate. They understand the Gambit Principle: sacrificing a piece now to secure a strategic position later. Great leaders think the same way.
They don't just manage time—they deploy it.

Here are four principles to help cultivate the Gambit Mindset:

1. **Define a long-term vision.**
   Be precise. Don't just say, "I want growth." Say, "In ten years, we'll lead our industry in X, serve Y markets, and be known for Z." This level of clarity now becomes the filter for decisions later.

2. **Align daily actions with that vision.**
   Ask yourself: Does this task support the future I'm building? If not, consider delegating it—or dropping it altogether. When the present becomes a servant of the future, time starts compounding in your favor.

3. **Be willing to say no to short-term sugar.**
   Quick wins feel good. But if they distract from strategic growth, they're just empty calories. The best leaders build staying power by feeding on purpose, not impulse.

4. **Think in compounding returns.**
   The best decisions don't always yield immediate results. But when you invest in systems, people, and brand with consistency, those investments begin to stack—and eventually snowball.

Elliot began leading differently.

He declined to match his competitor's price war. Instead, he doubled down on R&D and brand differentiation. He stopped approving every campaign and started empowering his VPs to lead. And on Thursday mornings? He blocked them out—non-negotiable—for vision work. Not planning. Not reacting. Vision.

It wasn't just about different decisions—it was about a different rhythm. Elliot realized his calendar had become the scoreboard. With each empowered leader, each blocked hour for vision, each choice to forgo urgency in favor of clarity—he was reclaiming time. Not just for himself, but for the business he now saw with sharper eyes. His mentor had offered a compass, but it was these moves that set the heading.

TOOLS FOR LONG-TERM THINKING

If urgency burns fuel, vision builds engines.

To make time work for you, you must stop treating it like a series of emergencies—and start treating it like capital. That requires *long-horizon thinking*. The following tools aren't just planning exercises—they're time-leverage mechanisms that help you create traction over years, not just days.

THE 10-YEAR PLAN

Most leaders overestimate what can happen in a year—and wildly underestimate what's possible in a decade. Ten-year thinking slows the mind down. It elevates strategy above tactics. And it moves you from playing defense with time to playing offense with intention.

- **Start at the end:** What does success look like ten years from now?
  Paint a vivid, specific picture of your desired future. Go beyond revenue numbers—describe your market position, team culture, customer impact, and legacy. This becomes your North Star, informing every major decision.
- **Reverse engineer the milestones:** What needs to happen in three, five, and seven years to get there?
  Break the vision into strategic phases. Each time horizon should have its own priorities, capabilities to build, and metrics to track—allowing you to measure momentum without losing sight of the big picture.
- **Identify what compounds:** Which systems, relationships, or assets become more valuable with time?
  Look for areas where early investment yields exponential return: leadership development, customer trust, brand equity, process automation. These are your flywheels— slow to start, but powerful once in motion.
- **Decide what to sacrifice:** Not everything can grow at once. What will you under-resource now for a bigger payoff later?
  Strategic patience requires trade-offs. You may need to delay expansion, pass on short-term opportunities, or endure slower growth in one area to free up resources for what truly matters long-term.

QUARTERLY STRATEGIC RESETS

Even a ship with a clear compass heading can drift in the fog of daily execution. That's why quarterly resets—ideally offsite and distraction-free—are essential. They give leaders and teams space to breathe, recalibrate, and realign with the bigger picture. These resets aren't about adding more to the agenda; they're about silencing the noise so clarity can rise.

- **Begin with vision** – revisit your 10-year plan.
  Restate the long-term destination. Anchor the meeting by reminding the team why you're building what you're building—and what success is supposed to look like a decade from now.
- **Measure the gap** – what moved forward this quarter, and what didn't? Conduct a candid review of progress. Celebrate what advanced the mission. Be honest about what stalled—without blame, just clarity.
- **Eliminate** – what no longer serves your strategy?
  Identify projects, processes, or habits that have outlived their usefulness. Make courageous decisions to clear the clutter so your energy can be redirected toward high-leverage work.
- **Adjust course** – where do you need to reallocate attention or capital? Strategy isn't static. As markets shift and new data emerges, be willing to pivot thoughtfully. Course corrections now can prevent course disasters later.

Elliot's team adopted quarterly off-sites. No screens. No fires. Just thinking time… together. And for the first time in a long time, they stopped feeling behind—and started getting ahead.

VISION BOARDS AND FUTURE MAPPING

Research from Dr. Gail Matthews at Dominican University suggests that people who write down their goals are 42% more likely to achieve them. Why? Because when we visualize success, we move it from the abstract to the actionable.

Visualization doesn't just inform the mind—it engages the heart. It creates emotional commitment, not just intellectual understanding.

- Map key milestones on a timeline and post it where your team can see. Create a visual roadmap that charts out major phases of your journey—product launches, team expansions, market entries, strategic hires. When your team sees the timeline every day, it subtly shifts thinking from "what's urgent" to "what's important."
- Write your future company story in present tense. "It's 20XX, and we've just expanded into Europe..."
  Storytelling in present tense makes the future feel real. By casting the vision in narrative form, you help your team emotionally inhabit it—and that emotional buy-in becomes fuel for strategic action.
- Revisit it monthly. Don't let it collect digital dust.
  A vision that gets buried in a slide deck is no vision at all. Schedule time to re-engage with it—review progress, refresh your narrative, and re-energize your team's connection to the future you're building.

One CEO we coached installed a "Future Wall" in the break room. It sparked daily conversations about long-term goals—and kept the vision alive in the mundane moments.

THE POWER OF PLAYING THE LONG GAME

Long-term thinkers don't ignore the present—they *anchor* it. They understand that each decision made today is either a deposit or a withdrawal against tomorrow. Every hour spent, every meeting called, every priority chosen—it's all shaping the future whether you realize it or not.

When you shift your mindset from short-term survival to long-term traction, something powerful happens: Urgency loses its grip. Time stops slipping through your fingers. You gain margin, clarity, and momentum with a purpose behind it.

This mindset doesn't eliminate pressure, but it does transform it.

> *When vision leads, the flames don't define you—they refine you.*
> *You stop measuring your days by how much you got done, and start measuring them by how much progress you made toward what matters most.*

Elliot learned this firsthand. It wasn't that the problems disappeared—but they no longer owned his calendar. Vision gave him a filter. Strategy gave him a cadence. And his time? It finally started working for him, not against him.

The chess master doesn't rush the game. He uses time as a weapon. So must you.

When you commit to the long game, you stop reacting—and start building. You stop running out of time—and start compounding it. And in that space, traction takes hold.

CALIBRATION QUESTIONS

1. Where in my leadership have I mistaken activity for progress?
   → *Invites reflection on whether my busyness is aligned with strategic vision.*

2. What would a clear, vivid 10-year future look like for me and my organization?
   → *Encourages my long-range thinking anchored in purpose and specificity.*

3. Which daily or weekly commitments could I restructure to serve long-term goals?

→ *Prompts my examination of habits, meetings, or routines that lack alignment.*

4. What quick wins or urgent demands have consistently pulled me off course?

→ *Surfaces patterns of distraction that sabotage my traction.*

5. Who on my team could take more ownership if I gave them the space to lead ?

→ *Pushes me to consider empowerment as a strategy for reclaiming time.*

6. Where have I delayed important strategic investments because they felt slow or uncertain?

→ *Reveals my avoidance patterns that sacrifice future ROI for present comfort.*

_____

_____

_____

_____

7. If I committed to quarterly strategic resets, what impact would that have on our momentum and clarity?

→ *Taps into the transformative power of rhythm and realignment.*

_____

_____

_____

_____

Momentum isn't achieved in a day— it's built by choosing, every day, to make time serve what matters most.

FINAL THOUGHTS

Momentum in life and business doesn't happen by accident. It's the reward of leaders who trade frantic motion for intentional direction—who refuse to let urgency steal their strategy.

That's the invitation of this chapter: to stop reacting and start architecting. To shift from "What can I get done today?" to "What am I building over time?"

Elliot didn't need a new to-do list. He needed a new lens. One that let him see his time not as a liability, but as leverage. The moment he reset his internal compass, everything began to shift—from how he led, to how his team aligned, to how his business started compounding real momentum.

The same is true for you.

You don't need more hours. You need a better relationship with the ones you already have. Define the future. Align your present. Build what lasts.

*Time won't wait. But it will work—
for those who learn to lead it.*

RECOMMENDED RESOURCES

1. **Traction** by Gino Wickman
   Wickman lays out a framework designed to help leaders clarify vision, gain traction, and build a healthy organization. His tools for vision casting, quarterly resets, and scorecard metrics offer a concrete system for turning time into traction. This book is especially valuable for readers seeking practical ways to align daily operations with long-term strategy.

2. **The Infinite Game** by Simon Sinek
   This book challenges leaders to move beyond short-term wins and embrace an infinite mindset focused on long-term purpose, adaptability, and legacy. It aligns directly with the chapter's core theme of thinking beyond quarterly results and leading with enduring vision. Sinek's framework invites readers to reorient time around what will matter most in the long run.

3. **Essentialism** by Greg McKeown
   McKeown urges leaders to cut through noise and focus only on what truly matters—a discipline necessary for long-view leadership. His framework supports the chapter's call to avoid reactionary leadership and concentrate on strategic priorities. This book helps readers resist the pull of the urgent in favor of the important.

4. **Good Strategy Bad Strategy** by Richard Rumelt
   Rumelt defines what real strategy looks like—clear goals, guiding principles, and coherent actions—versus the empty fluff many mistake for strategic thinking. This book supports the chapter's argument that thoughtful, long-

range decision-making is a skill that separates reactive managers from visionary leaders. It equips readers with the mindset and tools to lead with clarity and intent.

5. **Great by Choice** by Jim Collins
    Through detailed case studies, Collins shows how companies thrive during chaos by anchoring themselves to consistent long-term behaviors like the 20 Mile March. His research reinforces this chapter's lesson that strategic discipline and long-term focus outperform short-term improvisation. The book powerfully illustrates how time rewards steady, deliberate leadership.

6. **The Tim Ferriss Show** (Podcast)
    Ferriss interviews elite performers who often share how they built sustainable success by prioritizing systems, routines, and time leverage. Many episodes offer practical examples of the long-game mindset discussed throughout this chapter. Listeners will find inspiration and tactics for reclaiming their time and investing it with greater intentionality.

7. **Masters of Scale** (Podcast with Reid Hoffman)
    Hoffman's interviews with startup founders highlight how big ideas require long-term bets, clear vision, and resilience through setbacks. The show reinforces the chapter's contrast between reactive tactics and proactive, long-view leadership. It provides firsthand stories of how successful leaders use time to create scale.

8. **Measure What Matters** by John Doerr
    Doerr introduces OKRs—Objectives and Key Results— as a framework to help leaders track progress toward ambitious, long-term goals while staying nimble. His

approach provides a practical tool to bridge the gap between quarterly execution and decade-long vision. It's a resource every strategic leader can use to bring focus and accountability to their team.

9. **Good to Great** by Jim Collins
This classic explores what differentiates enduring, high-performing companies from their merely good counterparts. Collins introduces the concept of the "flywheel effect"— the idea that consistent effort in the right direction builds momentum over time. It aligns perfectly with this chapter's emphasis on compounding investments, long-term thinking, and the power of disciplined leadership.

10. **CEO Excellence** by Carolyn Dewar, Scott Keller, and Vikram Malhotra
Based on research of top-performing CEOs, this book shows that visionary thinking, clear priorities, and long-term orientation are consistent traits of exceptional leaders. It validates many of the leadership practices advocated throughout this chapter. The insights here help operationalize strategic patience and purpose-driven leadership.

11. **Radical Focus** by Christina Wodtke
Using a story-driven approach, Wodtke explains how to use OKRs to keep teams focused on long-term objectives while remaining agile in the short term. Her work supports the chapter's message that clarity and alignment are essential to executing a compelling vision. This book blends narrative and framework in a way that's both practical and inspiring.

12. The Long Game by Dorie Clark

Clark lays out a roadmap for resisting short-term pressure and building a meaningful life and career over time. Her frameworks echo the chapter's encouragement to embrace strategic patience and invest deeply in the future. It's an empowering read for any leader ready to trade urgency for intention.

20 | RECLAIMING TIME WILL CHANGE YOUR STORY

LEGACY THINKING

"I WISH I HAD SPENT MORE TIME AT THE OFFICE."

– NO ONE, EVER –
(at death's door)

THE FORK. THE PLATE. THE TRUTH.

Stephen didn't look like someone losing at life. On paper, he was winning. As the CEO of a high-growth tech company, he had built a reputation for being decisive, tireless, and endlessly available. His calendar overflowed with meetings, investor calls, strategy sessions, and team check-ins. His phone rarely left his hand. Most nights when he was home, dinner with his family was like one more piece in a calendar puzzle, trying to fit the moment in between overlapping obligations, and none of it getting his full, undivided attention.

He told himself it was temporary—just until they closed that next round, landed that next client, launched that new platform. The treadmill would slow down soon…

…but it never did.

Then came the moment that sliced through all his rationalizations.

It was a Tuesday. He had flown back early from a conference to make it home in time for dinner—a rare appearance. As he sat at the table scrolling through an urgent email thread, his six-year-old daughter gently tapped her fork against her plate. "Daddy," she asked without looking up, "why do you love work more than me?"

Time stopped.

Stephen's hand froze mid-scroll. His heart dropped, and for a moment, he forgot to breathe. He looked across the table at his wife, who had quietly moved her hand to her mouth, eyes welling with tears. His daughter kept her gaze fixed on her plate, waiting in silence for a response that choked in Stephen's throat.

The question landed like a freight train hauling every compromise, every broken promise, every missed recital, and every postponed family trip. But it wasn't just the present moment it uncovered. It reached backward.

Stephen flashed to his own childhood. His father—an accomplished entrepreneur in his own right—had launched multiple successful companies, but had rarely been home before bedtime. The man had provided everything... except presence. Young Stephen had spent countless dinners just like this one, noting the empty seat at the table and wondering if building a business meant forfeiting a family. He had promised himself then that he would never repeat that pattern.

And yet here he was.

The weight of generational repetition hit him like a wave. For years, he'd convinced himself that this grind was the price of achievement. That excellence demanded sacrifice. But looking now at his daughter's downcast expression, hearing her voice tremble with innocent clarity, he realized what was really at stake: her perception of his love.

That night, Stephen didn't sleep. He lay awake thinking about the hidden costs of his choices—not just the strain on his marriage or the growing distance from his child, but the erosion of his own well-being. The fatigue he wore like a badge. The anxiety that followed him from boardroom to bedroom. The friendships left uncultivated. The silence in his soul where joy used to live.

He knew something had to change. Not later. Not after the next big milestone. It had to change now, because "someday" doesn't come with a guarantee.

The next morning, he canceled every non-essential meeting. The ones he did attend had clear boundaries set in advance. He met with his leadership team one-by-one and began delegating decisions he had once clutched too tightly. What began as a course correction became a transformation. Stephen started reclaiming time—not to do less, but to live more.

He wasn't stepping back from success; he was redefining it. With each intentional choice, the clock slowly began to work for him, not against him.

THE ULTIMATE REWARDS OF MAKING TIME BEHAVE

Most professionals equate freedom with financial success. The bigger the paycheck, the freer the life—or so the thinking goes. But those who reach the upper rungs often discover a paradox:

> *Money without margin still feels like poverty.*

Time control isn't about squeezing more into every hour. It's about investing your hours where they yield meaning. It's the difference between being efficient and being fulfilled. High-functioning leaders who turn this corner discover that mastery over time allows them to reclaim something far more valuable than their inbox... their presence.

WHEN TIME CONTROLS YOU:

- **Your calendar answers for you.** Days fill up before you've even had a chance to consider what matters most. Saying "yes" becomes a reflex, and "no" feels like a moral failure—even when it's the wiser choice.
- **You wear long hours like armor.** Busyness becomes the proxy for worth. Instead of asking, "Did it matter?" you find yourself asking, "Did I do enough?"
- **Moments with loved ones feel like borrowed time.** You're physically present, but mentally distant. Laughter feels rare. Connection feels accidental.

- **Accomplishment comes with a side of anxiety.** Even your wins feel like something you have to survive. The pressure never lets up—because your pace is unsustainable, and deep down, you know it.

Stephen lived in that space for years—the limbo of "someday." The pivot came not from abandoning excellence, vision or duty but from identifying what was most important and choosing to align what mattered most to him with those values.

DESIGNING A LIFE THAT ALIGNS WITH YOUR VALUES

Time, and how you spend it, is the most honest mirror of what you truly value. It silently documents your deepest loyalties. You can declare that family, health, friendship, or faith are important, but your use of time tells the truth. And for many leaders, that truth is sobering. The gap between what we declared and what we actually do is wide enough to sail a cruise ship through.

Is it time for you to close that gap? Here's an approach to try:

1. **Define your true priorities.**Strip away the noise. If nothing was demanding your attention—no deadlines, no expectations—what would you pursue or protect? What rhythms would you fight to keep sacred? Your priorities become more real when you name them, not when you only feel them.
2. **Audit your time.**Covered in some detail by the earlier chapters, track how your hours are actually spent over the next fourteen days. Don't judge—just observe. You may feel some discomfort when you compare the results with your values. That's a good thing; discomfort is clarity in

disguise. If you want to keep-it-real, invite someone you trust to help hold you accountable to what your time audit is revealing.

3. **Define non-negotiable time blocks.**Some things shouldn't be penciled in—they should be chiseled in stone. Whether it's dinner with your kids, morning reflection, or a daily workout, guard these moments with the same ferocity you'd reserve for a board meeting... because they're worth more.

4. **Eliminate, automate, and delegate.**If a task doesn't require your wisdom, presence, or leadership, ask "why is it still cluttering my plate?" Efficient use of time isn't always about doing more—it can also be about doing fewer of the wrong things. Let go so you can grow.

5. **Set firm boundaries.** Not boundaries that are so stiff that they snap under pressure, but strong ones that bend with grace and stand with integrity. Work will always expand to fill your life unless you build firm walls around what matters.

As an aside, a 2024 Forbes article discussed "misalignment burnout," which occurs when individuals engage in activities that conflict with their innermost values and beliefs (see recommended resources below). This constant engagement in misaligned tasks can lead to chronic stress and eventual burnout.

THE MYTH OF "I'LL SLOW DOWN LATER"

One of the most pervasive lies in leadership circles is the myth of deferred life. The idea that you can burn the candle now and enjoy the glow later. That "hustle" is a season; That someday you'll arrive at "enough."

Perhaps you've played at this? (Haven't we all?)

- "After this quarter..." turns into next year.
- "Once we hire..." becomes "once we scale."
- "When I retire..." often arrives too late.

> *The dangling carrot tends to spoil*
> *before it can be eaten.*

CALIBRATION QUESTIONS

1. Where in my life do I currently spend the most time and energy—and does that reflect my deepest values?
→ *Encourages an honest audit of time allocation versus personal convictions.*

2. Where have I allowed urgent demands to crowd out my most important priorities?
   → *Prompts awareness of how reactive habits erode intentional living.*

3. What non-negotiable time slots do I need to establish—or reestablish—in my weekly calendar?
   → *Invites proactive design of margin, rest, or priority-driven commitments.*

4. What belief or fear is keeping me from delegating or eliminating low-impact tasks?
   → *Surfaces the internal narrative that protects busyness over effectiveness.*

5. How often do I say yes out of guilt instead of alignment with what matters most?
→ *Challenges people-pleasing patterns that compromise focus and energy.*

6. When was the last time I intentionally created margin for rest, reflection, or meaningful connection?
→ *Encourages pause to evaluate the pace and presence in life rhythms*

7. If I committed to quarterly strategic resets, what impact would that have on our momentum and clarity?
→ *Inspires vision for a calendar that reflects calling, values, and sustainability.*

> *Time doesn't tell the truth—*
> *until you ask it where it went.*

FINAL THOUGHTS

Freedom doesn't show up when the last email is sent or the final box is checked. It shows up when your calendar finally reflects what you've known at a soul-level all along—what matters most. You weren't made to drift from demand to demand, always reacting, always running and gunning.

You were made to lead, to build, and to steward your time like the precious, limited and irreplaceable resource it is.

This chapter wasn't about squeezing more productivity from your hours. It was about restoring authority to the one person responsible for how your time gets spent—you. When your schedule begins to serve your values, everything else—your relationships, your energy, your impact—starts to shift.

Don't just take control of your time. Take responsibility for the story it tells.

RECOMMENDED RESOURCES

1. **The Ruthless Elimination of Hurry** by John Mark Comer
   Comer presents a spiritual and practical antidote to the modern epidemic of busyness and overload. Drawing from the life of Jesus, he invites readers to slow down and reclaim a life of presence, peace, and purpose. This message reinforces the chapter's call to resist hurry and create space for what truly matters.

2. **At Your Best** by Carey Nieuwhof
   Nieuwhof helps readers identify and operate in their personal "green zones"—the times of day when their energy is highest. By syncing important tasks with peak energy and protecting margin, readers can achieve more by doing less. This book enhances the chapter's message of stewarding both time and energy.

3. **Win at Home First** by Cory M. Carlson
   This book challenges leaders to prioritize what truly matters—starting with the relationships under their own roof. Carlson speaks from experience, offering tools and reflection exercises to help high-performing professionals bring the same intentionality to their personal lives that they apply to their careers. His message echoes the heart of this chapter: success isn't real if it costs you the people you love.

4. **The ONE Thing** by Gary Keller and Jay Papasan
   Keller and Papasan introduce a focusing question that drives powerful clarity: "What's the ONE thing I can do such that by doing it, everything else will be easier or unnecessary?" The book offers practical tools to avoid

distraction and maximize impact through targeted action. It reinforces the chapter's emphasis on prioritization and focus.

5. **Mind Your Mindset** by Michael Hyatt and Megan Hyatt Miller
This resource explores how internal narratives shape our decisions, productivity, and leadership outcomes. The authors offer a practical framework for replacing limiting beliefs with empowering ones. It aligns with the chapter's encouragement to challenge time-scarcity mindsets and rewrite unhelpful assumptions.

6. **The Tim Ferriss Show** (Podcast)
Ferriss interviews top performers from a wide range of disciplines, deconstructing their routines, mental models, and time habits. The show frequently explores unconventional ways to reclaim autonomy over time and energy. Listeners can glean creative, high-leverage strategies for building a life that works by design.

7. **Focus on This** (Podcast by the Full Focus team)
This podcast walks listeners through practical applications of the Full Focus Planner system, developed by Michael Hyatt. Topics include goal-setting, weekly reviews, calendar blocking, and maintaining boundaries with intention. It's a tactical companion to the chapter's vision of purpose-driven time design.

8. **A Psychologist Explains 'Misalignment Burnout'** (Forbes.com)
This article introduces a concept called "misalignment burnout," which occurs when one's daily work consistently clashes with their deeper values. It reveals how time spent out of sync with purpose can lead to fatigue, cynicism,

and professional drift. The piece validates the chapter's challenge to align time with what truly matters.

9. **Work and Rest God's Way** by Scott LaPierre
   This book provides a biblical perspective on work-life balance, emphasizing rhythms of rest, purpose, and sabbath. LaPierre offers theological grounding for protecting margin and honoring God through both diligence and stillness. It supports the chapter's invitation to design life in alignment with faith and eternal values.

10. **Time Off: A Practical Guide to Building Your Rest Ethic** by John Fitch and Max Frenzel
    Fitch and Frenzel explore how rest is not a luxury, but a critical ingredient in creativity, clarity, and sustained performance. They present historical, scientific, and practical arguments for cultivating a "rest ethic" alongside a work ethic. This fresh angle deepens the chapter's call to create space for renewal, not just output.

11. **Slow Productivity** by Cal Newport
    Newport's latest book introduces the idea that doing fewer things better—and at a more sustainable pace—is the antidote to chronic overwhelm. He champions depth over speed and teaches readers how to reframe productivity in long-term, life-giving ways. It dovetails perfectly with the chapter's message about designing time with intentionality and margin.

12. **Life in the Rhythm of Grace** by Rebecca Lyons
    Lyons invites readers to embrace a lifestyle marked by rest, renewal, and alignment with God's purpose. Drawing from personal experience and biblical insight, she shares how to break free from hurry and reorient life around rhythms of grace. This book expands on the chapter's

spiritual undercurrent and challenges readers to structure their lives around what restores rather than depletes.

WHEN THE CLOCK STRIKES NOW

"THE LONGER YOU WAIT FOR THE FUTURE, THE SHORTER IT WILL BE."

- LOESJE -

Time doesn't knock politely.

It barges in with little warning, then disappears through the cracks while we're staring at screens, stuck in meetings, or chasing after someone else's urgency. One moment you're pouring your morning coffee, and the next... you're wondering how it's already Friday. Again.
But time isn't the real thief.

Distraction is. Disorganization is. Disconnection is. The real enemy is a kind of quiet drift that sets in when we stop leading our time—and start reacting with it.

That's why you picked up this book. Not just to get a few productivity tips. Not to feel more efficient. But because something in your soul knew it was time to stop settling. You're not just here to run a business or check boxes. You're here to steward something—a mission, a team, a calling, a life.

LET'S REWIND FOR A MOMENT

Over these past twenty chapters, you've done more than read. You've moved. You've taken a tour through the real-time trenches of leadership. We started by pulling back the curtain on the forces draining your focus—those unseen habits and mental reflexes that sabotage even the best intentions.

You confronted decision fatigue and reclaimed margin.

You named the cost of micromanagement—and loosened your grip. You exposed how digital noise was hijacking your clarity.

You learned that reactive calendars and scattered systems were undermining your influence, not just your productivity.

But you didn't stop there.

You made the shift from passive to proactive.

You started designing days that reflect your real priorities. You learned to protect peak energy hours, build deep work vaults, and align strategy with capacity. You created rhythms that serve you instead of enslaving you. And in doing so, you began something powerful:

You started making time behave.

Not perfectly. Not flawlessly. But differently.

And in the process, you began to realize that time mastery isn't about control—it's about congruence. It's about living a life that matches your values, fuels your purpose, and magnifies your impact. When time starts to mirror what matters, you don't just get more done—you become more of who you were created to be.

So... What Now?

If you've made it this far, then you're not just curious. You're committed.

But let's be honest: insight alone doesn't change anything. Not for long. Without action, awareness becomes self-help. You'll close this book with good intentions and drift right back into the grind.

Unless you decide to do something different.
Unless you install what you've learned. Embed it. Rehearse it. Share it. Recommit to it, not once, but again and again.

Because time will always drift toward disorder unless you lead it. That's where rhythm comes in. That's where review and reinforcement matter.

That's where community makes all the difference.

Leadership is lonely enough. You don't have to figure this out alone.

A PERSONAL INVITATION

If something in these pages stirred something in you—if you found clarity, conviction, or a sense of possibility you haven't felt in a while—then I'd love to invite you to reach out.

Not because I have all the answers. But because I've spent the better part of my life helping leaders like you find theirs.

At Bauer Leadership, we coach business owners, entrepreneurs, and high-level leaders who are ready to stop reacting and start architecting a life of greater purpose, presence, and peace.

We walk with you—step by step—to bring structure to your days, alignment to your calendar, and deeper satisfaction to the life you're building.

This is not a quick fix. It's a partnership. It's about stewardship, not shortcuts. But I promise you this: when you invest in building a life that reflects what matters most, time doesn't just stretch—it starts working for you.

So, if you're ready to do more than just read about change—if you're ready to live it—then let's talk.

You can email me at **support@timegambitbook.com** using "Let's Connect" in the subject line and a brief description of where you have identified a need for help.

Or even quicker, schedule a no-pressure call directly at: https://app.usemotion.com/meet/bwmbauer/ TimeGambitConnectCall And let's explore what's possible— together.

MAKE YOUR MOVE

The clock is still ticking.

You don't need another year of reactive hustle. You need a plan. A rhythm. A mindset. A partner.

You already made your first move by picking up this book.

Now it's time to make the next one.

The Time Gambit has begun.

Let's win back what matters most—starting now.

ABOUT THE AUTHOR

Brent Bauer is the founder and CEO of Bauer Leadership Consulting Group, a coaching and advisory firm dedicated to helping entrepreneurs, executives, and their teams design businesses that are profitable, scalable, and freeing. With over 30 years of leadership experience spanning corporate roles in Georgia, Florida, and Alabama—as well as significant contributions to nonprofit organizations—Brent brings a depth of perspective rooted in both strategic insight and hands-on execution.

Driven by a lifelong curiosity around what truly makes a leader worth following, Brent coaches clients to go beyond mere titles. For him, true leadership is about inspiring others to bring their best while consistently modeling authenticity, intention, and calm under pressure. Whether your current challenge is accelerating sales, empowering a winning team, improving cash flow, or preparing to exit your business, Brent's proprietary diagnostic tools and structured coaching approach are designed to deliver clarity, confidence, and forward momentum.

He leads with a servant-hearted philosophy—listening deeply, prioritizing organizational health, and investing in culture as the foundation of sustainable growth. And he practices what he preaches, integrating ongoing personal development and time mastery into his own life and work.

Brent holds a deep passion for helping high-capacity leaders reclaim their time without compromising their mission—

because he's lived it himself. He now helps others write that same story:

A legacy of impact, influence, and intentional living.

www.ingramcontent.com/pod-product-compliance
Lightning Source LLC
Chambersburg PA
CBHW070527090426
42735CB00013B/2881